The Reagan Paradox

The Reagan Paradox

THE CONSERVATIVE ICON AND TODAY'S GOP

BY LOU CANNON
AND TIME CONTRIBUTORS

INTRODUCTION BY JOE SCARBOROUGH

Published by TIME Books,
an imprint of Time Home Entertainment Inc.

Time Home Entertainment Inc.
1271 Avenue of the Americas, 6th Floor
New York, NY 10020

ISBN 10: 1-61893-383-3
ISBN 13: 978-1-61893-383-6

We welcome your comments and suggestions about TIME Books.
Please write to us at:
TIME Books
Attention: Book Editors
P.O. Box 11016
Des Moines, IA 50336-1016

If you would like to order any of our hardcover Collector's Edition books,
please call us at 800-327-6388 Monday through Friday, 7 a.m.–8 p.m.,
or Saturday, 7 a.m.–6 p.m., Central Time.

Contents

Introduction

A LEGACY OF OPTIMISM AND COMMON SENSE

BY JOE SCARBOROUGH

Former Florida congressman Joe Scarborough is host of MSNBC's
Morning Joe *news talk show and author of 2013's*
The Right Path, *about the current course of the Republican Party.*

THERE IS A WONDERFUL SCENE IN THE POPULAR 1980s movie *Back to the Future*. The film's plotline sends a teenager raised in the heart of the Reagan era back to the '50s. There, Michael J. Fox's character meets the younger version of the mad scientist, Dr. Emmett Brown, who built the time machine that transported him. To check Fox's bona fides, the scientist tests him.

"Then tell me, future boy, who's president of the United States in 1985?"

"Ronald Reagan," Fox answers.

"Ronald Reagan? The actor?" Christopher Lloyd's character laughs incredulously. "Then who's vice president? Jerry Lewis?"

All these years later, the joke continues to be on Ronald Reagan's skeptics and doubters. The man whose political skills were mocked by California's legendary governor Pat Brown and then by all the smart guys in the Carter White House made believers of those political rivals by rolling up historic electoral landslides in California and then the nation. Twenty-five years after he flew west on Air Force One for the last time, it is safe to say that millions of Americans would still love to go back to the future and have President Reagan in the Oval Office once again.

It is now 10 years after his passing, which is the occasion of this book. Looking back from this vantage point, Reagan's legacy remains vivid and potent. How else to explain how a conservative movement and political party continue to obsess over the question "Who is the next Reagan?" And as his Republican Party is slowly learning, it is a frustrating question and may, in fact, have no answer, because Ronald Wilson Reagan was unique.

It makes no more sense than for Democrats to search for the next Franklin D. Roosevelt or military leaders to seek out the next Dwight Eisenhower. These men possessed certain skills for their times that allowed them to bend history for all time. There is no guidebook for such greatness.

In law school we learned the Latin phrase *sui generis*, which means "of its own kind" or "unique in characteristic." Reagan was of his own kind. Reagan was unique. He believed in God, the American people and himself—and knew how to communicate those values in a way that no conservative has before or since.

Yet Reagan the conservative was a man as focused on America's glorious future as he was on preserving the values of the past. He was no reactionary. He was, instead, the iconic American who believed in what was yet to come. This had been the hallmark of American exceptionalism since Thomas Paine told his fellow citizens they could remake the world.

Those men who gathered in Philadelphia set a course for America that has always pointed toward the future. Along the way, our ship of state was violently tossed by slavery, a historically bloody civil war, a staggering depression and two world wars. But America was sustained by its people's inner strength and determined optimism. Men like Reagan continued to believe that the United States was headed toward a brighter future—until they hit the turbulence of the '60s and '70s, when the national identity felt tremors of doubt.

For a time, America stopped listening to her heart and her head. The wind was no longer in her sails.

In the span of 11 years, America lost a war and two presidents, one from an assassin's bullet and the other by his own failings. A third was driven from office, chased by the chants of "Hey, hey, LBJ, how many kids did you kill today?"

The social and moral polarity of the American universe was upended. The antihero had become the hero, and American soldiers, returning home from the lost cause of Vietnam, were spat upon. An oil embargo, 21.5% interest rates and a hostage crisis fostered a malaise that spread across the nation. I still remember my fifth-grade teacher telling my class that, as had befallen the seemingly invulnerable Roman Empire, America's days as a world power were quickly coming to an end.

Like my teacher, many believed Henry Luce's American Century was over, 20 years ahead of schedule.

Ronald Reagan was born for a time such as this.

He was a figure derided by the elites of both political parties, Wall Street, academia and the national media. They said he was too simple, too unqualified and too inexperienced to lead the free world. His ideas were antiquated, and they predicted that his foreign policy would push America into a third world war.

Yet the millions of Americans who carried Reagan to huge victories in 1980 and 1984 felt that this was a man who was uniquely qualified to lead the country back to greatness. Reagan, after all, had been a conservative star, a successful labor leader, a two-term governor running the seventh-largest economy in the world and, yes, a Hollywood actor. It would take all of the Gipper's on-screen skills to make his countrymen believe that the economy could be turned around, that the Soviet Union could be defeated, and that America's greatest days truly did lie ahead.

John Jay, Alexander Hamilton and James Madison, in pushing for the creation of a Constitution for the young country, argued that the most important considerations for a president were experience and character. The boy from northwestern Illinois had bushels of both.

He also had Nancy Reagan at his side, and she, as anyone who saw them together will attest, was his greatest treasure.

Ronald and Nancy Reagan won the White House by asking men and women from all corners of the country, including Democrats and independents, to join his "community of shared values." Unlike many in today's Republican Party, Reagan made an open appeal to Democrats on the campaign trail and at the GOP convention.

Reagan Democrats and independents answered his call for change. And then President Reagan changed the world.

My friend Craig Shirley, one of Reagan's leading biographers, told me, "Reagan bends light and thus changes the future. He changes American conservatism, he changes the Republican and Democratic parties, he changes America and he changes the world."

For Reagan, common sense was intellectualism. He also believed American conservatism was about challenging the status quo. Frederick Douglass, the great Republican abolitionist—whether addressing suffragettes in Washington, D.C., or a church congregation in Dundee, Scotland—summoned his lifelong rallying cry: "Agitate! Agitate! Agitate!"

Reagan and Reaganism were about agitating against the conventional wisdom of political parties and entrenched powers. The man who spent most of his life being mocked by Washington ended up changing it forever because, to paraphrase another Hollywood star, he frankly didn't give a damn what his elite critics thought of him.

Reagan is ubiquitous now in American politics, cited frequently by members of both parties, who all too often don't truly understand his brand of conservatism or the man himself. That makes the study of his life and times so vitally important.

Were his eight years in Washington defined by Hollywood glitz and glib politics? Certainly not. On occasion, did he compromise on such conservative touchstone issues as taxes, entitlement programs and immigration reform? Yes, but always with the longer view in mind. In the end, did he succeed? Consider this: America's victory in the Cold War freed tens of millions imprisoned by communism across the world. Twenty million new jobs were created at home. Double-digit inflation and interest rates were wiped away. Unemployment fell to around 5.3% by the time he left office, and, more important, America's national morale was restored.

Ronald Reagan had inherited a badly divided Republican Party and an even more fractured country, but as he flew west on the day of his retirement from national politics, he flew over a country more confident in its future than at any time since the 1950s.

John O'Sullivan of *National Review* observed that "the fact" of America would always exist, but it was "the idea" of America that the 40th president restored. Shirley points out that well over 1,000 books have been written about Reagan, but for historians, "the realm of Reagan scholarship is just opening up. There is enough of Ronald Reagan for all of us to breathe."

Some may be discouraged that there is no new Reagan on the horizon. But many, like myself, thank God that America got the leader it needed at precisely the right time and place.

Having him back might even be worth a Vice President Jerry Lewis.

The Practical Conservative

CASTING A LONG SHADOW EVEN TODAY

BY LOU CANNON

Lou Cannon covered Ronald Reagan while he was governor of California for the San Jose Mercury News *and was the senior White House correspondent for the* Washington Post *during Reagan's presidency. He has also published five books about Reagan's life and career.*

AGENERATION AFTER HE LEFT THE WHITE HOUSE and a decade after his death, the 40th U.S. president remains an elusive figure. The American people admire Ronald Reagan, ranking him in Gallup surveys with the martyred Abraham Lincoln and John F. Kennedy as one of the best presidents. Historians generally agree that Reagan's faith in America's future and his sunny approach to the presidency restored public confidence when the nation was adrift. Some go further: historian John Lewis Gaddis called Reagan one of the "saboteurs of the status quo" who helped bring the Cold War to a conclusion.

However, Reagan's place in history remains a matter of considerable dispute. In the political arena Republicans invoke his name more than they emulate his policies, while Democrats have grudgingly upgraded their evaluation of a president they once regarded as a menace or dismissed as an amiable dunce. Barack Obama said that Reagan "changed the trajectory of America" in ways that Richard Nixon and Bill Clinton did not. Despite such grace notes, Reagan's legacy is often undervalued or misunderstood. His harshest critics still dismiss him after all these years as an intractable right-winger whose bristling anti-Soviet rhetoric brought the world to the brink of war while he lowered taxes for the rich and shredded the social safety net. This caricature offered by the left is matched by a caricature on the right that also has a strained relationship to reality. In this version Reagan won the Cold War and dispatched the Soviet Union single-handedly while undercutting the welfare state and reducing America's dependence on government.

The facts make mincemeat of these comic-book histories. Reagan moved both right and left during his eight years in the White House, according to what he perceived as the needs of the nation. Some of what he did should be hailed as positive by both sides and some by neither. One thing for certain, however, is that everyone should be thankful that Reagan reached out to the Soviet adversary he had called an "evil empire," negotiating with Mikhail Gorbachev and transforming a relationship that had been mired in hostility and fear. Everyone should also take comfort from a bipartisan reform he initiated that extended the solvency of Social Security.

Income-tax reductions are a more disputed legacy, but Reagan lowered them for everyone and eliminated them for most of the poor. No one should be happy—even Reagan wasn't—that he allowed the national debt to soar. His immigration reform, cutting across party lines, has more champions among liberals than among conservatives. His Supreme Court legacy is a work in progress: his third appointee, Justice Anthony Kennedy, holds the swing vote on a closely divided court with many crucial issues yet to be decided.

When Reagan was alive, his admirers often said of him: what you see is what you get. While meant to praise, this simplified view diminishes Reagan, who had core values but a practical and competitive approach to politics that valued results more than rhetoric. This meant compromise, lots of compromise, and he did not shrink from it. During Reagan's presidency, his staff divided into rival camps of "pragmatists" and conservatives who called themselves true "Reaganites." He did not take sides in the labeling because he was simultaneously pragmatic and conservative. In the end, he achieved most of his major goals by compromising in ways that would seem anathema to today's Tea Party stalwarts. He succeeded because he was a practical conservative.

NUCLEAR ARMS AND THE COLD WAR

DURING REAGAN'S NEAR-MISS CAMPAIGN for the Republican presidential nomination in 1976, President Gerald Ford's strategists ran a commercial in California showing a hand reaching for the White House hotline, nuclear crisis in the air. The punch line, meant to frighten, declared: "Governor Reagan couldn't start a war. President Reagan could." President Jimmy Carter expanded on this theme in the 1980 campaign because his polls, like Reagan's, showed Reagan vulnerable on the war issue. This wasn't surprising considering Reagan's sometimes strident anti-Soviet rhetoric and his personal history of deep disdain for communism and its subversive agenda that "wantonly disregards human rights."

Ultimately, he feared and detested the existence of nuclear weaponry more than he did the Russians, and, in the single most significant achievement that defines his legacy, he ignored some top advisers' cautions and actively sought dialogue with the Soviet leadership. As a result, he set in motion events that would halt the runaway proliferation of nuclear arms and eventually lead to the end of a Cold War that had overshadowed American politics since the end of World War II.

Specifically, the Intermediate-Range Nuclear Forces (INF) Treaty signed by Reagan and Soviet leader Mikhail Gorbachev on Dec. 8, 1987, was the first accord to reduce U.S. and Soviet nuclear arsenals instead of stabilizing them at higher levels. It set the stage for future agreements that made even deeper reductions in these arsenals and established a once-unimaginable process of mutual verification. Inspectors from the United States and Russia now routinely examine nuclear facilities on each other's soil and, under the New Start Treaty signed by Obama and Vladimir Putin, will do so at least until 2021. As a result, the world is safer today because of Reagan and Gorbachev—and the Soviet Union no longer exists.

Would this have happened without Reagan? Was it all a matter of good timing or good luck? The authoritative Cold War historian Don Oberdorfer rejects the view that the Soviet Union was fated to collapse from internal weaknesses with a slight nudge. "Nowhere was it written in the stars that the heavily armed Soviet Union would pass away peacefully and that the attendant Soviet empire in Eastern Europe and Central Asia would pass into history with hardly a shot being fired," Oberdorfer wrote. "It is a marvel of history that the end of Soviet power came peacefully, bringing about the end of the Cold War.... With different decisions and different people, it could have turned out very differently for the United States and the Soviet Union, indeed, for all humankind."

The people at the helm were Reagan and Gorbachev, plus their deputies, U.S. Secretary of State George Shultz and Soviet Foreign Minister Eduard Shevardnadze. Gorbachev realized that his country was spending far more on military purposes than its creaky command economy could afford. Reagan, in office four years before Gorbachev assumed the reins of leadership, was well informed about conditions inside the Soviet Union and dubious of CIA estimates that he thought exaggerated Soviet capability. Demonstrating what Shultz calls "strategic thinking," Reagan advocated a military buildup that he believed would pressure the Soviet economy and prod the country's leaders to bargain on nuclear-arms reduction, with the United States negotiating from a position of strength.

For Reagan, unlike some Cold Warriors, the buildup was always a means toward this end. At the *Washington Post* on June 18, 1980, a month before his nomination as president, I invited him to the paper to meet the editors, and one suggested that the buildup could intensify the arms race. "I think there's every indication and every reason to think the Soviet Union cannot increase its production of arms," Reagan responded, adding that Russians were having a hard time getting "enough to eat."

The conventional wisdom in Washington when Reagan arrived was that the United States and the U.S.S.R. could perpetually avert nuclear war through the horrific logic of mutual assured destruction (neatly condensed to the telling acronym MAD). Since each nation could destroy the other, neither would go to war. Reagan rejected "this truly mad policy" as an invitation to disaster, understanding that superpowers could blunder into war through miscalculation or accident. He was aware of occasions in which one side or the other had been on the verge of a mistake that could have triggered World War III. One such incident, recounted by David Hoffman in his book *The Dead Hand*, occurred in 1983 when a faulty Soviet early-warning system reported a massive U.S. missile launch. A Soviet lieutenant colonel, operating on "gut instinct," decided the launch was a false alarm and kept the Soviet missiles in their silos.

Congress approved the Reagan military buildup, but it took time to bring results. During his first term, the Soviet Union had four leaders in less than three years. With the ascent of the younger and more robust Gorbachev, Reagan was delighted to finally have a negotiating partner, but he received no help from movement conservatives, who accused him of "moral disarmament." William F. Buckley joined such establishment Republicans as Nixon and Henry Kissinger in opposing ratification of the INF Treaty. The Senate ratified it overwhelmingly, with some senators ridiculing the notion that the anti-communist Reagan had gone soft on the Soviets.

In fact, he had put to good use a negotiating approach that he had learned years before in a much smaller but still challenging setting. He led the Screen Actors Guild in a difficult strike and in 1960 hammered out an agreement with Hollywood movie producers that obtained residual fees for actors. Interviewing Reagan after his first meeting with Gorbachev, I asked him what was most neglected in his biography. Negotiating for the Screen Actors Guild, he said. And what had he learned from this effort? "That the purpose of a negotiation is to get an agreement," he replied.

MILESTONES ON THE HOME FRONT

REAGAN'S DOMESTIC ACHIEVEMENTS were considerable and strategic—and they helped him in his negotiations with Gorbachev. He wanted a strong economy for its own sake but also believed it would show the Soviets that the United States would have the long-term edge in any military competition. Although Obama is now challenged by a Republican-controlled House, the Democratic House majority in the first two years of his presidency enabled him to win passage of his controversial health-care bill. By contrast, Reagan faced a House controlled by the opposition during his entire eight years in office. He nonetheless advanced his agenda on a number of contentious issues through negotiation and compromise—and by exerting pressure on vulnerable Democrats.

Despite concern in some quarters that his vocal criticisms of government would translate into an attack on New Deal entitlements, Reagan preserved them. He was the last president to extend the solvency of Social Security. He named a commission chaired by Alan Greenspan that blended Democratic and Republican proposals, taxing high-income recipients and gradually raising the retirement age. Commission members were appointed by the president, Democratic House Speaker Thomas P. (Tip) O'Neill and Republican Senate leader Howard Baker. Watching Reagan sign these amendments to the Social Security Act in a White House ceremony on April 20, 1983, O'Neill called it "a happy day for America."

Reagan was the last president to obtain substantial tax reform. The Tax Reform Act of 1986 ended the historical system of taxing capital gains at lower rates than ordinary income. It also freed about 7 million low-income Americans from paying federal income taxes, beginning a trend in which nearly half the adult population—Mitt Romney's belittled 47%—now pay no such tax.

Reagan was the last president to provide amnesty for immigrants who had entered the United States illegally. The Immigration Reform and Control Act of 1986 that he proposed and signed into law made 3 million such immigrants legal residents of the United States.

He also supported and signed in 1988 the U.S.-Canadian Free Trade Agreement, the precursor to the North American Free Trade Agreement (NAFTA), signed into law by President Clinton five years later.

Even on issues on which his overall record was less than sparkling, Reagan made some constructive differences. Cass R. Sunstein, writing in the *New York Times*, called him "an environmental hero" for being "the prime mover behind the Montreal Protocol, which required the phasing out of ozone-depleting chemicals."

Reagan also appointed 382 federal judges, more than any other president. As described by Terry Eastland, a participant in the process, the Office of Legal Policy established by Attorney General William French Smith reached beyond "the country-club lawyers that populate the Republican Party to include law professors and others who have actually thought about the law." The American Bar Association, generally considered a bastion of liberal thought, gave 54% of Reagan appointees its two highest ratings, a better mark than his four predecessors, Carter, Ford, Nixon and Johnson.

Reagan filled three vacancies on the Supreme Court, making choices that reflected diversity without entirely fulfilling his oft-proclaimed and unrealizable goal of naming justices who would interpret the law rather than make it. In 1981, carrying out a campaign promise, he made history by naming Sandra Day O'Connor the first woman on the court. Reagan was so charmed by her that he did not interview anyone else and accepted at face value O'Connor's statement that she was personally opposed to abortion. (Reagan hardly ever pressed on this issue; he opposed abortion as the taking of a human life, but throughout his presidency he addressed the annual pro-life rally in Washington by telephone so he was never seen on television with its leaders.) The Senate confirmed O'Connor unanimously, despite opposition from social conservatives who accurately suspected she was pro-choice.

Reagan's next appointment was Antonin Scalia, the first justice of Italian-American descent, also confirmed unanimously. But Reagan's third choice, Robert Bork, a conservative with political baggage, was rejected in 1987 by the Senate, then in Democratic hands. The fight was so bitter that "Bork" endures as a Senate verb, used whenever the opposition is accused of distorting the record of a presidential nominee.

But Reagan recovered from the Bork loss with his appointment of Anthony Kennedy, who had a dependable conservative record on a lower court and was the swing vote in his first term on a decision that narrowed *Roe v. Wade*, the landmark ruling legalizing abortion. But justices change over time, and Kennedy moved from the right of the court to the center on some issues—and to the left of center on gay rights. On the last day of the 2003 court session, Kennedy's 6–3 majority opinion in *Lawrence v. Texas* overturned an anti-sodomy law and said the 14th Amendment protected "intimate, adult consensual conduct." A prominent social conservative denounced Kennedy as "one of the most dangerous men in America." He remains the swing vote on a conservative court.

Not all of Reagan's domestic policies were beneficial. In 1981 he made counterproductive budget reductions in the WIC (Women, Infants and Children) program, which provides pre- and postnatal care for mothers. Congress restored most of the money, and Reagan's budget expanded the program in 1988.

Almost all of his economic achievements came at a dear price. William Niskanen of his Council of Economic Advisers praised Reagan for lowering tax rates but tartly questioned the existence of a genuine Reagan Revolution that, as promised, would reduce the size and cost of the federal government. Along with other conservative economists, Niskanen was disappointed that the Reagan economic program increased budget deficits and the national debt. The budget is a barometer of a president's priorities, and Reagan never once in eight years submitted a budget that paid for all the programs he thought necessary. "The American people are conservative," columnist George Will said presciently at the outset of the Reagan administration. "What they want to conserve is the New Deal." Reagan did, but at the price of perennial unbalanced budgets—also a feature of the New Deal.

THE GREAT COMMUNICATOR

REAGAN IS SOMETIMES REMEMBERED LESS for his practical deeds than for his words. But those words would become a vital element of his legacy, drawing their persuasive potency from what the political scientist Hugh Heclo calls Reagan's "sacramental vision of America," as was set forth in a speech Reagan called "America the Beautiful":

> *I, in my own mind, have always thought of America as a place in the divine scheme of things that was set aside as a promised land. It was set here and the price of admission was very simple; the means of selection was very simple as to how this land should be populated. Any place in the world and any person from these places; any person with the courage, with the desire to tear up their roots, to strive for freedom, to attempt and dare to live in a strange and foreign place, to travel halfway across the world, was welcome here. And they have brought with them to the bloodstream that ... precious courage ... to strive for something better for themselves and for their children and their children's children. I believe that God in shedding his grace on this country has always in this divine scheme of things kept an eye on our land and guided it as a promised land for these people.*

Reagan could have delivered this speech when he was president. He actually gave it in 1952 when still a Democrat. It was a commencement address at William Woods College in Fulton, Mo., just a mile from Westminster College, where, six years earlier, Winston Churchill had warned that an "iron curtain" was descending over Eastern Europe. Registering Republican in 1962, Reagan would go on to serve two terms as governor of California and two terms in the White House, and in all that time, the romantic view of American exceptionalism he had displayed in Fulton never wavered.

Reagan expressed that view with quiet eloquence, avuncular charm and even humor—a winning combination with the American public. Even his most hard-edged speeches were sprinkled with self-deprecating humor. After being shot 10 weeks into his presidency, he looked up at the surgeons about to operate and said, "I hope you're all Republicans."

Reagan came up with most of his one-liners and, until he became governor of California in 1967, wrote his own speeches. He appreciated good writing and assembled a talented team of White House speechwriters, often editing what they wrote. He was a particularly empathetic and comforting mourner-in-chief, as he demonstrated on Jan. 28, 1986, in expressing the nation's grief for victims of the space shuttle *Challenger* disaster. He had an ear for the dramatic phrase, and an actor's flair. "Mr. Gorbachev, tear down this wall," he said in Berlin on June 12, 1987, his voice rising to be heard above loudspeakers trying to drown him out from the East German side of the Brandenburg Gate. "Reagan's mellifluous rhetoric lingers like a melody that evokes fond memories," George Will wrote after Reagan's passing.

The 40th president deflected such plaudits—as anyone who knew him would expect. In Reagan's telling, both his rhetorical gifts and the accomplishments they helped effect were reflections of the American people. In his farewell speech from the Oval Office on Jan. 11, 1989, after noting that he was often called "the Great Communicator," Reagan said: "But I never thought it was my style or the words I used that made a difference: it was the content. I wasn't a great communicator, but I communicated great things, and they didn't spring full-blown from my brow. They came from the heart of a great nation—from our experience, our wisdom, and our belief in the principles that have guided us for two centuries. They called it the Reagan Revolution. And I'll accept that, but for me it always seemed more like the great rediscovery, a rediscovery of our values and our common sense."

HIS ROOTS AND REVOLUTION

SINCE REAGAN GREW UP A DEMOCRAT in the depths of the Great Depression, it is no surprise that Franklin D. Roosevelt, Democratic architect of the New Deal, was his early idol and a shaping force of his political style. Like FDR, Reagan wanted to make Americans believe in themselves again, and largely did. The oldest U.S. president in history was convinced that the nation's best days were still to come. "America has a rendezvous with destiny," he said, quoting Roosevelt.

In 1932, just out of college, the 21-year-old Reagan landed his first job as a radio announcer, in Davenport, Iowa. The following year he was so mesmerized by FDR's inaugural address that, on air, he recited from memory the president's famous declaration, imitating his upper-class accent: "We have nothing to fear but fear itself—nameless, unreasoning, unjustified terror which paralyzes needed efforts to convert retreat into advance." As president, Reagan emulated the conversational speeches FDR called "fireside chats" and made the Saturday radio speech a weekly institution.

Reagan's expressed debt to FDR went beyond radio. The New Deal put his hard-luck father, Jack, jobless and alcoholic, to work distributing relief funds in Lee County, Ill. As noted Reagan biographer Garry Wills discovered, Reagan's brother, Neil, was given a similar if lesser job, although in the Great Depression two family members were rarely allowed on the federal payroll.

Even when Reagan drifted to the right in the 1960s and criticized President Lyndon Johnson and other Democrats, he remembered what FDR had done for his family and never disparaged him. In 1980, accepting the presidential nomination in Detroit, he concluded by quoting from FDR on the need for efficiency in government as baffled Republicans on the convention floor fell silent.

Gratitude is a powerful emotion, but there was more to Reagan's positive view of FDR than appreciation for the jobs the New Deal provided his father and brother. He admired Roosevelt as a doer, in peace and war. When World War II broke out, Reagan was an actor in Hollywood and an Army reservist. Disqualified from combat because of nearsightedness, he spent most of the war near home in Culver City, narrating Army training films. He was thrilled when his voice and FDR's were used together in a 1942 film, *Beyond the Line of Duty*.

Reagan was a sophomore at Eureka College in 1930, studying economics, when a Republican-controlled Congress passed the Smoot-Hawley law, imposing the highest tariffs in U.S. history on imported goods. His economics professor blamed the Great Depression on these tariffs, and the lesson stayed with Reagan. Both as Democrat and Republican, he supported free trade and opposed protectionism. That view would be enriched by reading the free-market economists Milton Friedman and Friedrich Hayek. But his deepest convictions on economic issues, particularly taxes, arose from personal experience.

Reagan had not grown up wealthy. He often said his family in Dixon, Ill., didn't live on the wrong side of the tracks but was close enough to hear the train whistle. He started out at minimum scale in Hollywood, but his career took off in 1940 when he landed the role of the doomed Notre Dame football player George Gipp in *Knute Rockne—All American*, a part that gave Reagan the enduring nickname "the Gipper." Then the 1942 film *Kings Row* led to a million-dollar contract from Warner Bros. After the war, when the marginal income-tax rate exceeded 90%, he was well paid—and highly taxed—for the first time in his life. He subsequently became a lifelong advocate of low income-tax rates.

As governor of California in 1967, he raised taxes to close an inherited deficit, but in 1973 he pushed an initiative that would have written tax limitations into the state constitution. Voters rejected it. In 1978, after he was out of office and contemplating a presidential run, California voters passed Proposition 13, a sweeping tax-limitation initiative that sparked a national antitax movement. One of the leaders was Rep. Jack Kemp, a former professional football player who represented a Buffalo, N.Y., district and had once been an intern for Governor Reagan.

Kemp was the principal author of the Kemp-Roth bill, a 1978 tax-reduction measure that attracted national backing from conservatives. Reagan warily endorsed Kemp-Roth but expressed private concerns that tax cuts, combined with the defense-spending increases he proposed, would produce a budget shortfall. Supply-side economists—and Kemp—assured Reagan that reduced tax rates would foster a cornucopia of economic growth, resulting in more revenues than if rates were left unchanged. Reagan gave in.

Again like his hero FDR, Reagan avoided grubby economic details. Indeed, in 1980 he relied more on history than on economics—and more recent history than the New Deal. Reagan recalled that President John F. Kennedy had proposed tax cuts to stimulate the economy under the theory that "a rising tide lifts all boats." Reagan liked the sound of that. He also agreed with Kemp that cutting taxes for everyone—and eliminating them entirely for the poor—would blunt Democratic accusations that Republicans cared only for the rich. Without ever proclaiming himself a supply-sider, Reagan made income-tax cuts a major promise of his presidential campaign.

The Republican establishment that celebrates Reagan today did everything it could in 1980 to keep him out of the White House. George H.W. Bush denounced Reagan's tax-cut plan as "voodoo economics." Howard Baker suggested that Reagan, then 69, was too old. Bush won the Iowa caucuses, but Reagan bounced back in New Hampshire, where he memorably rose to the occasion in a Nashua debate after a pro-Bush moderator tried to silence him. Paraphrasing a line from a Spencer Tracy movie, Reagan declared, "I paid for that microphone," and went on to win the debate, the primary and the nomination. He then united his political party by choosing Bush as his running mate.

His campaign to unseat President Jimmy Carter was waged against the backdrop of Americans held hostage since Nov. 4, 1979, at the U.S. embassy in Tehran, but Reagan said little about Iran. His strategist Stuart K. Spencer told him the election would turn on economic issues, as it did. Carter was stung by an especially telling, and oft-repeated, Reagan rhetorical question, a variant of a line from an FDR fireside chat: "Are you better off than you were four years ago?" Most Americans weren't.

Reagan went on to defeat Carter in an electoral landslide, inheriting a U.S. economy that was in its worst shape since the Great Depression. When he took the oath of office on Jan. 20, 1981, the United States was suffering from double-digit inflation, with the Consumer Price Index registering 11.3% in 1979 and 13.5% in 1980. The prime rate, the lowest rate for commercial borrowing, was 21.5%.

Presidents are blamed for whatever happens on their watch, but the economy was suffering from structural deficiencies well before the Carter presidency. For two decades after World War II, the U.S. economy dominated a world in which every other industrial power had been destroyed or economically exhausted. But by the time Nixon became president in 1969, foreign competition had revived, while the U.S. economy suffered from "stagflation"—stagnation in growth combined with an inflated cost of living. Nixon imposed wage and price controls, which failed. So did various tactical maneuvers by Gerald Ford and Carter.

Reagan decided on a more daring and enduring course. Echoing George Shultz on Reagan's foreign policy, economist John B. Taylor said Reagan took a "strategic approach" toward the economy. On February 18, 1981, the White House submitted to Congress a 281-page message, "America's New Beginning: A Program for Economic Recovery," which would become better known as Reaganomics. It proposed:

- A budget-reform plan to cut the rate of growth in federal spending
- A series of proposals to reduce personal income-tax rates by 10% a year over three years and to create jobs by accelerating depreciation for business investment in plants and equipment
- A far-reaching program of regulatory relief
- In cooperation with the Federal Reserve Board, a new commitment to a monetary policy to restore a stable currency and healthy financial markets

Broadly speaking, these points synthesized Reagan's economic thinking as it had evolved over a quarter-century. "The Reagan economic program, like the Reagan constituency, reflected a range of views on economic policies," Niskanen wrote in his book *Reaganomics*. "For the traditional Republicans, a lower growth in federal spending was a necessary complement of any reduction in taxes … for the new 'supply-siders,' a reduction in tax rates was necessary to induce the economic growth that would permit a lower growth of the federal spending."

What was missing was mention of a balanced budget. Reagan had run on it in 1980, but by 1983 it had been reduced to "a personal dream." As much as Reagan wanted to believe otherwise, a balanced budget was incompatible with other priorities of Reaganomics.

UNINTENDED AFTERMATH OF A SHOOTING

FORTUNE FAVORS THE BOLD, AND REAGAN had luck on his side at the beginning of his presidency. As he delivered his inaugural address, the American hostages in Iran were freed after 444 days in captivity. Reagan was happy for the hostages and their families—and relieved. As presidential counselor Edwin Meese III explained, Reagan would have been forced to divide his energies between the economy and the hostages had they remained in captivity. Instead, as White House chief of staff James A. Baker III put it, "We have three goals, and all three of them are economic recovery."

The administration maintained this focus until March 30, when Reagan gave a speech at the Washington Hilton that ended with a favorite quotation from Thomas Paine: "We have it in our power to begin the world over again." Leaving the hotel through a side exit, Reagan paused to hear a reporter's shouted question. He was greeted with gunfire. John Hinckley, a 25-year-old drifter who was undergoing psychiatric treatment, had infiltrated the press photographers' area and fired six shots, wounding four people. White House press secretary James Brady, with a bullet in the brain, was the most seriously injured. Reagan had been shot, too, although he at first didn't realize it. Secret Service agent Jerry Parr shoved him into the presidential limousine. On the way back to the White House, Parr saw a trickle of blood coming from Reagan's mouth and diverted the motorcade to George Washington Hospital. Parr's quick thinking may have saved Reagan's life. He was bleeding internally from a bullet that had lodged within an inch of his heart.

Reagan survived his wounds, endearing himself to the nation in the process. "Honey, I forgot to duck," he said to Nancy Reagan at the hospital, in words attributed to fighter Jack Dempsey after he lost his heavyweight title to Gene Tunney in 1926. Reagan's near-miss with mortality had reminded him of favorite movie

lines—and his political heroes. "All in all I'd rather be in Philadelphia," he wrote on a notepad in the recovery room, reprising
W.C. Fields's dig at his hometown. In another note he quoted
Winston Churchill: "There's no more exhilarating feeling than
being shot at without result."

The shooting, in fact, had significant unintended results. It
produced an outpouring of public sympathy, which helped Reagan get his economic program through Congress. But it slowed
his learning curve on foreign policy and may have contributed
to subsequent overdelegation of authority to a zealous National
Security Council staff. Most important, Reagan's courageous
quips removed any doubts that he was a cardboard man whose
emotions were as synthetic as a celluloid screen. He had already
shown an abundance of charm in the first 69 days of his presidency.
"When he displayed that same wit and grace in the hours after
his own life was threatened," wrote *Washington Post* columnist
David Broder, "he elevated these appealing human qualities to
the level of legend."

In his hospital bed, Reagan looked up at Jim Baker, Ed Meese
and Michael Deaver and asked, "Who's minding the store?" The
three men, known as the troika, would later have differences, but
they worked smoothly together after the shooting in conveying
to the world a sense of business as usual inside the White House.
Reagan returned to the public stage on April 28, speaking to a
joint session of Congress about his economic program. He began
by reading from a letter written by a Maryland second grader:
"I hope you get well quick or you might have to make a speech
in your pajamas."

The speech was a hit, but Reagan still needed Democratic votes
to get his economic program through the House. He sought them
from the Southern Democrats known as Boll Weevils, led by
Charles Stenholm and Phil Gramm. White Southern Democrats,
rare today in Congress, were plentiful in 1981. But Reagan had

carried their districts against Carter, and the Boll Weevils realized they could be turned out in the next election. Baker, a Texan
like Gramm and Stenholm, suggested to Reagan that he promise
not to campaign in 1982 against any House member who voted
for both his tax and budget bills. Reagan embraced the idea.

He lobbied members of Congress relentlessly, holding 69 White
House meetings that 467 members attended in the first 100 days
of his presidency. He also compromised, yielding to demands
from four Louisiana House members to revive an expensive sugar
subsidy that had been phased out in 1979. Reagan's budget director, David Stockman, thought restoration of the sugar subsidy
scandalous and disliked other congressional add-ons, including
a tax giveaway to the oil industry. But the White House could not
have won without them. Gramm-Latta, a spending bill that was
the most closely fought of three measures containing the economic
program, passed the House by only six votes.

The final version of the economic program reduced income
taxes by 25% over three years, but the House had attached so many
tax breaks for corporations and so many pet spending projects for
members that the budget deficit ballooned. Reagan reluctantly
agreed the following year to roll back some of the reductions. The
1981 economic package also cut the marginal tax rate from 70%
to 50%. Five years later, the Reagan tax-reform bill would further
reduce the marginal rate to 28%.

Gramm-Latta passed on June 26, with supply-siders predicting a quick economic turnaround. Instead, the economy plunged
into recession. But along with economic problems, Reagan had
inherited part of the solution in the imposing person of Paul
Adolph Volcker, the Carter-appointed chairman of the Federal
Reserve Board. At their first meeting Reagan asked Volcker why
the Federal Reserve was needed, and Martin Anderson, who was
present, said Volcker nearly swallowed his cigar. But the Fed chairman recovered and patiently explained the vital role of a central

bank to the nation's economy.

To the surprise of many, Reagan met regularly with Volcker at the White House and became a staunch defender of the Fed chairman. Carter had pressured Volcker to impose credit controls, which failed and were soon scrapped. Reagan told Volcker he should do what he thought was right.

In their stubborn defiance of polls and politics, the president and the Fed chairman turned out to be kindred souls. Volcker proposed to strangle inflation by reducing the money supply and forcing up interest rates. This strategy also pushed up joblessness and made Volcker a vilified poster child: the cover of *Tennessee HomeBuilder* magazine depicted him and other Fed governors in a wanted poster, charging them with "premeditated and cold-blooded murder of millions of small businesses" and the kidnapping of the American dream.

TURNING THE TIDE OF RECESSION

IN TERMS OF DOMESTIC POLICY, THIS WAS Reagan's finest hour. The worse the recession became, the more he vowed to stay the course. "Our administration is cleanup crew for those who went on a nonstop binge and left the tab for us to pick up," he told a New York audience on Jan. 14, 1982, when surveys by pollster Richard Wirthlin put his approval ratings in the mid-30s. "The recession hurts. It causes pain. But we'll work our way out of it."

It wasn't easy. He was picketed, editorially denigrated and pressured by Republican leaders worried about the 1982 midterm elections. "Volcker's got his foot on our neck, and we've got to make him take it off," Senate leader Howard Baker told confidants. But Reagan, again thinking strategically, looked beyond the midterms. He continued to back Volcker, who had become a folk hero on Wall Street, and in 1983 reappointed him. It was a deserved vote of confidence in the man whose firmness had rescued Reaganomics, which had become a term of derision during the recession. As the economy rebounded in November 1982, Reagan observed of his critics, "They don't call it Reaganomics anymore."

Recovery came too late for some Republican members of Congress. House Republicans lost 27 seats, but the GOP held the Senate, which it had won in 1980 on Reagan's coattails. Reagan was philosophical about the losses, all the more so as the recession turned into the most powerful economic recovery in U.S. history.

The numbers tell the story. The Reagan recovery that started in November 1982 lasted to July 1990, when George H.W. Bush was in the White House. This was 92 months of growth, surpassing the previous peacetime record of 58 months. The economy grew by a third. The stock market almost tripled in value. More than 20 million new jobs were created. The unemployment rate, 7.6% when Reagan took office and 9.7% at the height of the recession, dropped to 5.3%.

Most satisfying for Reagan (and Volcker) was the inflation rate. It was 13.5% when Reagan was elected and 4.8% when he left office—and continued to fall after that. It is the most enduring Reagan economic legacy; annual inflation has never risen above 3.8% from 1992 to the present day. But against this must be weighed the national debt, which soared from almost $1 trillion to $2.6 trillion—it is $17 trillion in the fifth year of the Obama presidency—and a corresponding increase in federal budget deficits.

As for President Kennedy's "rising tide," economic growth lifted most boats, if not all, during the Reagan years. The poverty rate increased a percentage point to 15.2% from Reagan's inauguration through the recession, then declined to 12.8% at the end of his presidency. Eighty-six percent of the poorest 20% of Americans enjoyed an increased standard of living. Overall, the recovery made Americans feel better about themselves and their country. It enabled Reagan to run for reelection in 1984 under the feel-good slogan "Morning Again in America." He carried every state except Minnesota, plus the District of Columbia. It may not have been morning for everyone, but for most Americans it was at least the dawn.

In summary, Reagan fulfilled two of the three big promises he made in the 1980 campaign, reducing taxes and increasing military spending—both at the expense of his third promise: to balance the budget. But that understates what he accomplished. The military-spending boost was intended to bring about U.S.-Soviet negotiations and end the Cold War. When the Soviet military threat diminished, Reagan's successors cut the U.S. military budget by 23%. That enabled President Clinton and a Republican Congress led by House Speaker Newt Gingrich to balance the budget for the first time since the Eisenhower years.

TRAGEDY IN LEBANON

IN CONTRAST TO HIS ACCOMPLISHMENTS with the Soviet Union and the economy, Reagan floundered in the Middle East. Few U.S. presidents have done well in a region afflicted by persistent sectarian and religious rivalries, as well as the intractable Israeli-Palestinian conflict. Still, though history set a low bar for Reagan, he did not clear it. There are three reasons for that.

The first is that neither he nor his two secretaries of state demonstrated the strategic thinking shown in Reagan's Soviet policy. Instead, he and his State Department reacted to events in the Middle East and failed to heed warnings of trouble to come. The second is that Reagan's cabinet was irreconcilably divided between those willing to use force to advance U.S. policy objectives in the region and those disinclined to risk American troops in limited engagements. Ironically, it was the secretary of defense and the Joint Chiefs of Staff, heeding what they considered the lessons of the Vietnam War, who preferred diplomacy, and the diplomats who were more apt to be warriors. The third reason is that Reagan proved indecisive, often wavering between the two camps.

It didn't help that his foreign policy was slow off the mark. The president was out of sync from the beginning with Alexander Haig, his first secretary of state, who never understood that Reagan did not want him determining the administration's foreign policy. On April 24, 1981, Reagan, over Haig's objection, lifted the grain embargo against the Soviet Union that Carter had imposed in 1979 after the Soviet invasion of Afghanistan. The same day, Haig tried to stop Reagan from sending a handwritten letter to Soviet leader Leonid Brezhnev that said that lifting of the embargo could lead to a "meaningful and constructive dialogue which will assist us in fulfilling our joint obligation to find lasting peace." In 1982 Haig lost Reagan's confidence when he assured him that the ongoing Israeli invasion of Lebanon was limited to securing a safe zone in the southern part of the country. By June, Israeli troops under Ariel Sharon's leadership had reached Beirut. Reagan accepted Haig's resignation on June 25, 1982, confiding to his diary that "this has been a heavy load."

Shultz, the new secretary of state, inherited a tumultuous situation. Reagan, who had considered Israel a trustworthy ally, was disgusted with what was happening in Lebanon. Israel's 10-week siege culminated with its planes bombing West Beirut for 11 consecutive hours on Aug. 12. At Deaver's suggestion, Reagan called Israeli prime minister Menachem Begin. "Menachem, this is a holocaust," Reagan said.

"Mr. President, I think I know what a holocaust is," Begin replied in a sarcastic voice.

Reagan refused to give ground, bluntly telling Begin he had to stop the bombing. Twenty minutes later Begin called back, saying he had ordered Sharon to halt the attacks. Reagan thanked him, hung up and said to Deaver, "I didn't know I had that kind of power."

But that was the high point of Reagan's impact in Lebanon, which soon became a trap for the United States.

Two days after the Reagan-Begin conversation, Syria announced its willingness to withdraw its troops and Palestine Liberation Organization forces under its command from war-torn Lebanon. Under a plan devised by a U.S. special envoy, 800 Marines joined French and Italian military units in overseeing the evacuation. Defense Secretary Caspar Weinberger told Reagan he was concerned about the safety of the Marines, and on Sept. 10, 1982, Reagan withdrew them to nearby ships over the objection of Shultz.

On Sept. 14, nine days before he was to assume the presidency of Lebanon, Christian leader Bashir Gemayel was killed by a powerful bomb during a speech. Israeli troops entered West Beirut and stood by as Gemayel's vengeful militia entered Palestinian refugee camps at Sabra and Shatila and massacred more than 700 people, many of them women and children. Reagan watched televised reports of this atrocity in the White House family quarters.

In contrast to his coolly rational approach to U.S.-Soviet relations, Reagan too often let his heart rule his head in the Middle East. Sickened by the killings at Sabra-Shatila, he brushed aside the warning of John Vessey, chairman of the Joint Chiefs, who said Lebanon was "the wrong place" for U.S. troops, and on Sept. 20 he sent the Marines back into Lebanon as part of a new multinational force with the ambitious mission of restoring a strong central government and evacuating foreign troops. There they stayed while Amin Gemayel, the unpopular brother of Bashir, was installed as president of Lebanon and Syrian ruler Hafez Assad plotted to remove him. Assad had ties with the radical Shia faction Hezbollah, which was suspected of killing Bashir and was determined to drive the United States from Lebanon. Meanwhile, in Israel, public opinion turned against the war. Sharon was replaced with Moshe Arens, who sought to bring Israeli forces home.

Hezbollah made its presence known on April 18, 1983, when a van filled with explosives destroyed the U.S. embassy in Beirut, killing 63 people, including 17 Americans. This should have led to withdrawal of the Marines, but Reagan, lacking consensus in his quarreling cabinet, left them in place as Israeli forces withdrew. After the Israelis pulled back, the 24th Marine Amphibious Unit at the Beirut airport came under near-constant artillery fire from Syrian-backed militias.

Then, at 6:22 a.m. on Sunday, Oct. 23, a smiling young man with a bushy mustache drove a Mercedes truck through the parking lot of the four-story headquarters where members of the First Battalion, Eighth Marine Regiment, were sleeping. In the words of the official report: "The truck drove over the barbed and concertina wire obstacle, passed between two Marine guard posts without being engaged by fire, entered an open gate, passed around one sewer pipe barrier and between two others, flattened the Sergeant of the Guard's sandbagged booth at the building's entrance, penetrated the lobby of the building and detonated while the majority of the occupants slept. The force of the explosion ripped the building from its foundation. The building then imploded upon itself."

Of the 350 servicemen in the building, most of them Marines, 346 were casualties. The death toll, including those extricated from the wreckage who later died, was 241, the worst loss of U.S. troops in any single incident since the battle of Iwo Jima in World War II. Soon afterward, another bomb exploded in West Beirut, bringing down a nine-story building and killing 58 French paratroopers.

Reagan was asleep in the master suite of the Eisenhower Cottage at the Augusta National Golf Club, where he was spending the weekend, when national-security adviser Robert McFarlane awakened him to tell him about the calamity. Reagan would remember it as the "saddest day of my presidency, perhaps the saddest day of my life." He told me in 1990 he blamed himself, saying, "Part of it was my idea—a good part of it." Shultz, a Marine combat veteran of World War II and champion of the deployment, was also shaken. At a meeting of the National Security Council after the Beirut bombing, he said, "If I ever say send in the Marines again, somebody shoot me."

On Oct. 23, 1983, there was no time for such reflection. The day before, the Organization of American States, a group of six former British colonies, had requested U.S. military aid to restore "peace and stability" in Grenada, where a renegade faction of Premier Maurice Bishop's Marxist party had taken control of the government and murdered Bishop. Reagan had previously been warned by Caribbean leaders that Grenada was becoming a communist beachhead; Cuba was building a 10,000-foot runway on the island that the president had suspected could be used to deliver arms to the Sandinista government in Nicaragua.

When he returned to Washington on Oct. 24, Reagan quickly approved plans for what turned out to be the briefest war in U.S. history. Marines landed on Grenada's western shore, and U.S. Army Rangers parachuted onto the southeastern tip of the 133-square-mile island, encountering antiaircraft fire and ground resistance from Cuban soldiers and members of the labor battalion building the runway. U.S. forces subdued the outnumbered Cubans in two days, captured Bishop's killers and found an immense cache of arms. U.S. casualties were 19 killed and 115 wounded in a force of 5,000, while 59 of the 800 Cuban defenders were killed and 25 wounded. The rest surrendered and were returned to Cuba.

MORE CRISES IN THE MIDDLE EAST

THIS QUICK LITTLE WAR HAD CONSEQUENCES on U.S. policy in Lebanon. Polls taken immediately after the bombing of the Marine headquarters showed overwhelming public disapproval for a continued U.S. presence in Lebanon. But Grenada changed the equation. The U.S. victory, accompanied by the rescue of 800 American medical students in the island nation, was cheered by the public and diverted attention from Lebanon. While the

Marine survivors tunneled underground and "lived like moles," in the words of the U.S. defense attaché in Beirut, Reagan and Shultz resolved to keep them in Lebanon and did for nearly four months. Shultz told a Senate committee it would be devastating to "cut and run" from Lebanon. Reagan picked up the phrase, using it in a radio speech from Camp David on Feb. 4, 1984. He said there was "no reason to turn our backs and cut and run. If we do, we'll be sending one signal to terrorists everywhere. They can gain by waging war against innocent people."

Even as Reagan spoke, the Gemayel government in Lebanon was disintegrating under military pressure from Shia militias. The surge of patriotic pride that had sustained the Reagan administration after Grenada faded with the collapse of the Lebanese government, and polls soon showed that a majority of the American people wanted the Marines out of Lebanon. What Shultz called "pullout fever" raged in Washington, where White House chief of staff James Baker struck up a rare alliance with Weinberger in seeking the withdrawal of the Marines. The secretary of defense commissioned an investigation of the bombing and picked a respected admiral, Robert Long, to head it. The Long report blamed Marine commanders for lax security but said the administration had relied too heavily on military options without "clear recognition" of changing political conditions or the threat of terrorism—as Weinberger had long contended.

Armed with the findings, Weinberger seized his chance. On Tuesday, Feb. 7, while Reagan was speaking in Las Vegas and Shultz was flying to Grenada, Weinberger made the case for pulling out the Marines to a National Security Planning Group meeting. It was presided over by a hitherto invisible ally, Vice President George H.W. Bush, a World War II combat veteran who saw no point in risking the lives of additional Marines. Bush was close to Baker, his former campaign manager, and had discussed the Lebanon situation with him. After the meeting was over,

Bush phoned Reagan and told him the NSPG had agreed that the Marines should be "redeployed." Reagan, whose only role in the decision was to ratify it, reluctantly assented. He would never use the word "withdrawal."

More challenges in the Middle East lay ahead. On June 14, 1985, TWA Flight 847 took off from Athens bound for Rome with 153 passengers and crew, including 135 Americans. Hijackers forced the pilots to fly to Beirut, where they beat and shot to death U.S. Navy diver Robert Stethem, dumping his body on the airport tarmac. The plane was refueled, flown to Algiers and then back to Beirut. Most passengers were released in one city or the other, but 39 passengers and crew were held as hostages in Lebanon, most under control of the Shia leader Nabih Berri. The hijackers were not mindless terrorists. Their goal was to force Israel to free 700 Shias who had been captured during the Israeli invasion of Lebanon and imprisoned in Haifa. They had struck at the United States because lax security at international airports made Americans vulnerable.

Privately, Reagan seethed at the murder of Stethem, but Israel was willing to release the Shia prisoners, so Reagan opted for diplomacy. The American hostages were released two days later after Reagan telephoned Assad and after national-security adviser McFarlane told Berri he would be held accountable if any hostages were harmed.

While the TWA hostages were still in custody, Reagan met in Chicago with their families, who were joined by two brothers of Father Lawrence Jenco, a priest held hostage in Lebanon since Jan. 8, 1985. The brothers bluntly pressed the president for action to free the priest. The interrogation was so painful for Reagan that the son of a TWA hostage said to him, "Mr. President, I don't know how you can stand your job."

Jim Baker would never have exposed Reagan to such questioning, knowing how emotional the president was about the hostages.

But Reagan at the beginning of his second term had unwisely allowed Baker to switch jobs with Treasury Secretary Donald Regan. The change was proposed by Regan, who wanted to be nearer the center of power. Mike Deaver, the president's closest aide, had wanted promotion to chief of staff. When he didn't get it, he left to become a lobbyist, while Meese succeeded William French Smith as attorney general.

Reagan was now without the troika that had stood staunchly at his side during the first term. Adequate at Treasury, Regan and the assistants he brought with him were in over their heads at the White House. Inexplicably, none recognized the importance of first lady Nancy Reagan or realized that the president often used her as a sounding board. Cut off from the information she needed to be effective, she complained that Regan "liked the sound of 'chief' but not of 'staff.'" Reagan, who valued harmonious working conditions, found himself surrounded by aides he barely knew and a chief of staff who quarreled with his wife.

This change came at a time when Reagan was increasingly frustrated by the persistent difficulty of dealing with terrorists beyond U.S. reach. On June 18, when asked about the TWA hijacking, Reagan said that any U.S. retaliatory action that might kill civilians would be "an act of terrorism in itself." As fate would have it, the next day Salvadoran guerrillas attacked a sidewalk café frequented by off-duty U.S. servicemen in San Salvador. Thirteen people were killed, including four U.S. Marines. Reagan's political advisers urged retaliation, but when McFarlane said that any raid would cause large-scale civilian casualties, Reagan decided against it. Few presidents have been as concerned about civilian deaths. In 1988, as the United States maneuvered to oust Panamanian strongman Manuel Noriega, Reagan vetoed an invasion plan he said would cause heavy casualties, as happened when Panama was later invaded at the orders of President George H.W. Bush.

Only twice in his eight years as president did Reagan retaliate against terrorist attacks. The first was against a strictly military target a few weeks after the bombing of the Marine headquarters in Lebanon. On Dec. 4, 1983, a day after U.S. reconnaissance aircraft were fired upon over Syria, Navy planes were ordered to attack Syrian antiaircraft emplacements—with unfortunate results. Two of the 28 American planes were downed, and a pilot was killed. The next retaliation occurred on April 14, 1986, when U.S. bombers struck the Libyan cities of Tripoli and Benghazi in response to the bombing of a West Berlin disco that had killed two American servicemen. The planes dropped 60 tons of bombs; two bombs hit the barracks of Libyan strongman Muammar Gaddafi, killing an adopted infant daughter. Gaddafi, said to be sleeping in a tent outside, was unscathed. The raid killed scores of civilians, and Reagan declined to authorize follow-up attacks.

THE IRAN-CONTRA SCANDAL

IRAN-CONTRA, WHICH BROKE INTO PUBLIC view in late 1986, is conventionally viewed as the seminal scandal of the Reagan presidency, which I find debatable. In terms of its human costs, Iran-contra had far less impact than the disastrous second deployment of the Marines to Lebanon. Reagan could not, of course, have foreseen the bombing of the Marine headquarters, but he had been warned by Weinberger and the Joint Chiefs that the Marines were in considerable danger.

However one comes down on this, there's an undeniable relationship between Lebanon and Iran-contra, and, once again, the president would miscalculate. In Lebanon, militants with presumed ties to Iran held seven Americans as hostages, and Reagan was keen on finding a way to free them. Iran and Iraq were then at war, and U.S. policymakers feared that an Iranian victory would interrupt the flow of oil from the Persian Gulf. Starting in 1983 the United States, under a program known as Operation Staunch, urged other nations not to sell weapons to either combatant—helping Iraq, which had ample Soviet weapons. As this policy became effective, Iran and Iranian exiles flooded the CIA with offers to exchange intelligence information for weapons.

These offers intrigued William Casey, the U.S. director of central intelligence. He was concerned with the fate of William Buckley, the CIA station chief in Beirut who had been kidnapped on March 16, 1984, and was one of the seven Americans being held in Lebanon. Casey feared that Buckley was being tortured to reveal the names of CIA agents in the region. Meanwhile, McFarlane explored a novel proposal that would supply U.S. weapons to a shadowy group of supposed "moderate" Iranians in return for help in securing the release of the hostages.

Shultz and Weinberger urged Reagan to reject this initiative. Weinberger told the president that selling weapons to Iran would violate U.S. export law; Shultz said the proposal would "negate the whole policy" of not making deals with terrorists. The secretary of state realized that if hostages became currency, kidnappers would capture even more of them. But Reagan was blinded to these sensible policy considerations. Intimates of the president told me that Reagan vividly imagined the plight of the hostages and thought it was his duty to rescue them. On Jan. 17, 1986, he signed a document approving McFarlane's covert initiative; Reagan wrote in his diary that he had agreed to sell antitank weapons to Iran.

Nothing good came of this fantastic scheme. McFarlane soon resigned as national-security adviser after conflicts with Don Regan but continued to work on the initiative from home. McFarlane's successor, John Poindexter, turned over operational details to Oliver North, a swashbuckling Marine lieutenant colonel on the National Security Council staff. On May 25, McFarlane, North and George Cave of the CIA flew to Tehran from Tel Aviv in an unmarked Israeli 707 loaded with antiaircraft spare parts. They bore gifts of pistols and a chocolate layer cake decorated with a brass key—plus maps for intelligence briefings on Iraq that Cave, against his wishes, had been ordered by Casey to share with the Iranians.

The plane landed and waited an hour on the runway before an Iranian arms buyer showed up with a detachment of Revolutionary Guards who unloaded the spare parts, took the gifts and ate the cake. McFarlane had been told he would meet with high-ranking Iranians, but the U.S. delegation spent four days in Tehran without ever seeing an important official. In fact, the "moderate Iranians" were fiction; the entire operation had been orchestrated by the Iranian government.

Reagan was heartened on July 26 when a blindfolded Father Jenco was released on the side of a highway. But as Shultz had foreseen, the covert initiative provided more incentives for kidnapping hostages than releasing them. Three Americans were taken hostage in Lebanon in September and October. After 500 antitank weapons were delivered to Iran at the end of October, three hostages were freed—and three other Americans kidnapped in January 1987. A year after Reagan approved the arms deal, there were still seven hostages being held in Lebanon. Two of the original seven had died, Buckley from medical neglect and Peter Kilburn, a former librarian at the American University in Beirut, murdered in apparent retaliation for the U.S. raid on Libya.

On Nov. 3, 1986, the Iran initiative was disclosed by a Lebanese magazine. The U.S. media cautiously picked up the story, not wanting to jeopardize a mass release of hostages the president believed was imminent. When this didn't materialize, Reagan tried to explain his actions on Nov. 13 in a nationally televised speech that was based on inaccurate information supplied by Poindexter.

Reagan had told me years earlier that television was a demanding medium that exposed those who were untruthful or inaccurate.

A *Los Angeles Times* poll the next day found that only 14% of those who heard the speech believed Reagan.

Worse was to come in the revelation of a covert subplot devised by Oliver North. Attorney General Meese was assembling a chronology of the initiative when he learned that a search of North's office had produced an April 4, 1986, memo from North to Poindexter containing a sentence that said $12 million of the proceeds from the arms sales had been earmarked to "purchase critically needed supplies for the Nicaraguan Democratic Resistance forces."

These forces were better known as the contras, a covert, CIA-run guerrilla force authorized by the White House in 1981 to pressure the Marxist government of Nicaragua. Reagan ardently supported the contras, whom he had once described as "the moral equivalent of the Founding Fathers." He never persuaded the Democratic-controlled Congress, which twice cut off funding to the contra forces.

Meese realized immediately that a secret diversion of funds to the contras raised the possibility that Reagan could be impeached. The attorney general interviewed Ollie North, who lied, saying the money had gone from the Iranians to the Israelis. But when Meese asked if the arms shipments were a trade for the hostages or had a strategic purpose, North told the truth. "It always came back to the hostages," he said.

And that, it turned out, was what enabled the Reagan presidency to survive, because the American public empathized with the hostages even while disapproving of arms sales to Iran. On Nov. 25, 1986, Reagan acknowledged he had authorized the arms sales but denied knowledge of the diversion of proceeds to the contras. He fired North, accepted Poindexter's resignation and named a bipartisan review board to investigate the arms sales. Congress launched a broader inquiry.

A federal court appointed Lawrence Walsh, who had prosecuted racketeers in New York, to conduct a criminal investigation. Walsh found that Reagan had participated or acquiesced in covering up the scandal but concluded that there was "no credible evidence that the president authorized or was aware of the diversion of profits from the Iran arms sales to assist the contras ..." But Walsh's finding wasn't issued until seven years later, on Aug. 4, 1993, when Bill Clinton was in the White House and Reagan was beginning to slip away into the mist of Alzheimer's disease. (Some of Reagan's key advisers were convicted of such charges as withholding evidence but were later pardoned by George H.W. Bush.)

In the holiday season of 1986, Reagan was disconsolate and adrift, stung by public rejection of his inadequate explanations and not knowing where to turn. Nancy Reagan stepped up to the plate. She had been kept in the dark on the arms deal, but she understood her husband and knew he couldn't function without public trust. The way to regain this trust, she told him, was to apologize to the American people.

She brought Deaver back to the White House to argue for an apology. When her husband didn't budge, Nancy Reagan turned to Robert Strauss, a former Democratic Party chairman who had once passed up a chance to tell Lyndon Johnson that the Vietnam War was destroying his presidency. Strauss told himself afterward that if he ever had another such chance, he would speak truth to power—and he told Reagan an apology was necessary. Reagan respected Strauss but still found it hard to admit he had been wrong. His wife didn't let up, however, and Reagan finally agreed to give the speech that restored his presidency. Nancy Reagan picked the deft speechwriter Landon Parvin to draft it.

"A few months ago, I told the American people I did not trade arms for hostages," Reagan told the nation on March 4, 1987, in words written by Parvin. "My heart and my best intentions still tell me that's true, but the facts and the evidence tell me it is not."

This wasn't quite a full-bore apology, but it proved to be enough. Reagan's approval ratings rose steadily after the speech, and he left the White House two years later with the highest ratings of any president who finished his term in office.

SUCCESS WITH THE SOVIETS

WITH THE IRAN ARMS SALES BEHIND HIM and harmony restored to the White House by the replacement of Regan with Howard Baker, Reagan again turned his focus to the Soviet Union. Throughout the sunshine and shadows of his presidency, he had nourished the hope of mapping a path to peace with a Soviet leader. This had often seemed wishful thinking. Nothing came of the conciliatory letter he had written to Brezhnev while recuperating from being shot in 1981. U.S.-Soviet relations languished, then worsened. Reagan's provocative rhetoric seemed at odds with the pursuit of peace—on March 8, 1983, he called the Soviet Union an "evil empire" and "the focus of evil in the modern world"—and U.S. arms-control strategy was hampered by interagency conflicts that Reagan did not resolve. But at least the United States had only one president. The Soviet leaders, as Reagan put it plaintively, "kept dying on me." Brezhnev died in 1982. He was succeeded by Yuri Andropov, a former head of the KGB.

Relations were strained again on Sept. 1, 1983, when a Korean Air Lines jumbo jet with 269 people aboard, including 61 Americans, wandered into Soviet airspace and was shot down by a Soviet fighter, an act Reagan called "a crime against humanity." A war scare developed in Europe, where French President François Mitterrand compared the situation to the Cuban Missile Crisis of 1962.

In November the United States and its NATO allies launched a routine test of communications and command procedures for nuclear weapons. A Soviet intelligence chief in London who secretly worked for British intelligence reported that KGB units were telling Moscow that the exercise was preparation for a NATO attack on the Soviet Union. Tensions further heightened on Nov. 22 when the West German Bundestag approved the deployment of U.S. Pershing and cruise missiles to counteract nuclear missiles the Soviets had installed in Eastern Europe. Shultz told me for this essay that he considered the Bundestag vote the turning point in the Cold War.

At the time, however, many thought the Bundestag action a step toward conflict. The day after the vote, the Soviets broke off missile talks in Geneva amid denunciations from both sides aimed at European public opinion. The Soviet press compared Reagan to Adolf Hitler. TIME captured the gravity of the situation by choosing Reagan and Andropov as men of the year, featuring them on the magazine cover standing back to back. But Reagan had already realized it was necessary to step back from the brink. In an interview for the magazine's story, he said he would no longer describe the Soviet Union as the "focus of evil"—and never again did.

He'd done more than that already, although the world didn't know it. Reagan was at his California ranch at the time of the KAL 007 incident. When he returned to Washington for a meeting in the Situation Room, Weinberger, CIA chief Casey and national-security adviser William P. Clark urged Reagan to take a hard line. Shultz, however, said it was important not to overreact, and the president agreed. "The world will react to this," Reagan said. "It is important that we not do anything that jeopardizes the long-term relationship with the Soviet Union."

It would take two more Soviet leaders for the relationship to take root. Andropov died from kidney ailments on Feb. 9, 1984, and was succeeded by a member of the Soviet old guard, Konstantin Chernenko, who was suffering from emphysema. Chernenko died on March 10, 1985, and was succeeded by Gorbachev, then 54, who had earlier traveled to London and charmed Margaret

Thatcher. "I like Mr. Gorbachev," she told Reagan. "I think we can do business with him."

These words would resonate as Reagan and Gorbachev sounded each other out at Geneva in 1985, then explored ridding the world of nuclear weapons at Reykjavik in 1986, signed the INF Treaty in Washington in 1987 and celebrated what Reagan called a "new era" in U.S.-Soviet relations in Moscow in 1988. In an extraordinary scene, Reagan stood before a marble bust of Lenin at Moscow University and extolled the virtues of freedom to a rapt student audience. As Gorbachev's biographers wrote, the Russians loved it.

None of this was as easy as a summary makes it sound. Reagan's collaborators in ending the Cold War—the other "saboteurs of the status quo," in historian Gaddis's phrase—included Thatcher, Polish leader Lech Walesa and Pope John Paul II. But Reagan was the point man. His summits with Gorbachev were marked by repeated disagreements and unpublicized exchanges that resulted in the release of Soviet dissidents and others held against their will in the Soviet Union. The key to these releases was that Reagan could never discuss them. As for Gorbachev, he was at times on a short tether, distrusted by the Soviet military establishment. To reassure his generals, Gorbachev stridently opposed the Strategic Defense Initiative, the antimissile shield proposed by Reagan that Gorbachev claimed was an attempt to develop "space weapons." Although it was never scientifically feasible, says the physicist Sidney Drell, it exerted pressure on the Soviets and helped produce the INF agreement.

The significance of SDI was not its military potential—either for offensive or defensive purposes—but the strain it put on the Soviet economy. SDI was not a single system. It was a research project involving an array of new technologies, some beyond Soviet capabilities.

Reagan walked away from the Reykjavik summit after Gorbachev insisted on limiting SDI to the laboratory. Both sides at first considered the meeting a failure, but as Don Oberdorfer observed in his book *The Turn*, Reykjavik "paradoxically would become a turning point in the relations between the United States and the Soviet Union." The two sides had come so far in their discussions before the summit collapsed that the outline of the treaty to eliminate medium-range missiles in Europe and Asia had emerged. Looking back on Reykjavik after the Cold War had ended, the Soviet deputy foreign minister, Alexander Bessmertnykh, gave Reagan much credit. "If it were not for Reagan, I don't think we would have been able to reach the agreements in arms control that we reached later," he said. "He really thought we should do away with nuclear weapons. Gorbachev believed in that. Reagan believed in that. The experts didn't believe, but the leaders did."

Reykjavik and the INF Treaty led to the end of the Cold War. "In addition to reductions in nuclear arsenals, other changes brought on by the end of the Cold War are equally striking," said Jack F. Matlock, a Russian-speaking Foreign Service officer who advised Reagan on Gorbachev and became U.S. ambassador to the Soviet Union. "Eastern Europe is free and so are the former Soviet republics; Russians have freedom of travel, a large measure of freedom of speech and other personal freedoms they did not have before. Markets opened in Eastern Europe and Asia."

When Reagan died in 2004, his old negotiating partner flew to Washington to pay his respects. As Gorbachev passed the casket lying in state, he caressed it tenderly. A few nights later at the Russian embassy, Gorbachev eulogized America's 40th president, whom he described as "an extraordinary political leader" who had "restored America's self-confidence." Reagan dedicated his second term to the task of being "a peacemaker," Gorbachev added, at the right moment in world history—when Gorbachev was leader of the Soviet Union. "Our interests coincided," he said.

"For him the American dream was not just rhetoric," Gorbachev said. "It was something he felt in his heart. In that sense he was an idealistic American."

Reagan was indeed idealistic, but he had another quality that contributed as much to his success: enormous practicality. He skillfully practiced the art of politics—defined by the historian Richard Hofstadter as the "craft of maneuver"—while rejecting the label "politician" because he believed it a negative one in the eyes of the American people. When I once referred in an article to Reagan as a "master politician," he remonstrated, telling me he wasn't really a politician at all but had just been using common sense. He may have had a point. Reagan had core values. He knew where he wanted to take the country. It was a combination of vision and common sense that made him an effective leader. It's why he casts such a long shadow.

Letters

Reagan writes about the nation and the presidency

AMERICANS 'ARE READY TO SAY "ENOUGH"'

June 27, 1959, to Vice President Richard Nixon about economic speeches Reagan made as a host and speaker for General Electric Theater

DURING THE LAST YEAR PARTICULARLY, I have been amazed at the reaction to this talk. Audiences are actually militant in their expression that "something must be done." The only adverse opinion in the last two years was an editorial in a local "teamster union" paper which I accept as further evidence that sound thinking is on our side.

In several instances this talk was broadcast and here too the reaction as evidenced by mail was unanimous in support of "sound economy." I am convinced there is a groundswell of economic conservatism building up which could reverse the entire tide of present day "statism." As a matter of fact we seem to be in one of those rare moments when the American people with that wisdom which is the strength of democracy are ready to say "enough."

'WE USED OUR POWER TO REBUILD'

April 24, 1981, to Soviet General Secretary Leonid Brezhnev, insisting that the U.S. had no imperialistic ambitions

IN YOUR LETTER YOU IMPLY that such things have been made necessary because of territorial ambitions of the United States; that we have imperialistic designs and thus constitute a threat to your own security and that of the newly emerging nations. There not only is no evidence to support such a charge, there is solid evidence that the United States when it could have dominated the world with no risk to itself made no effort whatsoever to do so.

Letters courtesy of the Ronald Reagan Presidential Foundation and Library

When WWII ended the United States had the only undamaged industrial power in the world. Our military might was at its peak—and we alone had the ultimate weapon, the nuclear bomb with the unquestioned ability to deliver it anywhere in the world. If we had sought world domination who could have opposed us?

But the United States followed a different course—one unique in all the history of mankind. We used our power and wealth to rebuild the war-ravaged economies of all the world including those nations who had been our enemies. May I say there is absolutely no substance to charges that the United States is guilty of imperialism or attempts to impose its will on other countries by use of force.

'GOVERNMENTS CAN'T SHUT DOWN'

Circa September 1981, to a woman whose son was fired in the wake of the air-traffic controllers' strike

I CAN UNDERSTAND your concern and heartache. I can only hope that you will understand why it isn't possible for me to reinstate all those who went on strike. The law specifically prohibits public employees from striking. As you say, striking "is an inalienable right"—but not for government employees....

When public employees began unionizing, organized labor at the highest levels supported their efforts only on the condition that they provide in their constitutions they would not strike. A strike is an economic contest between labor and management when negotiations have failed to resolve an issue. But governments can't shut down the assembly line. The services provided to the people, who in this case are the employers of all of us in government, must be continued....

We have an obligation to those who did stay on duty and who have maintained flying schedules up to 75 or 80 percent of normal. At the same time however I do feel a very real sorrow for those who followed the union leadership at such a sacrifice.

NOT 'ROBBING THE POOR'

Nov. 4, 1981, to a Kentucky woman challenging his economic priorities and White House renovations

YOU ASKED HOW WE could balance the budget by robbing the poor and giving to the rich. Well that isn't what we're doing. We are trying to reduce the cost of government.... We are reducing tax rates across the board....

We have not suggested reducing Social Security. We are trying to do what you suggested—removing those who are not disabled or deserving of grants they are presently getting.

We are not cutting back on school lunches for the needy. We are trying to quit providing them for those who aren't needy.

Now as to the White House, we aren't spending a penny of tax money. The government provides $50,000 for an incoming president to do what he will to the White House. We gave that money back to the government. We found, however, that the White House was badly in need of painting inside, the plumbing was so old there was danger of it giving way. Drapes and much upholstery was in need of recovering and replacing, etc. Friends started a campaign to get donations to have this work done. It has all been completed without spending a single tax dollar.

'THE UNSUNG HEROES'

Dec. 1, 1981, to a Florida man about spending and tax cuts

I HAVE JUST ANSWERED a young black woman separated from her husband, four children, thirty-three years of age who is on welfare, but has managed to get herself a high school diploma, and now is setting out to get off welfare and be self-sufficient. Her courage and her faith in this country as expressed in her letter were such that my own faith was renewed, if that were necessary. Actually, I've never lost faith....

People like yourself are the backbone of his country, the great middle class, the unsung heroes who get up in the morning and go to work, send the kids to school, pay their bills, and, yes, if war comes, send their sons, or go themselves if they're young enough. And it's true, they are the people who have been hardest hit by the ill-advised government policies of the last few decades. They are the people we're listening to and trying to help.

'ELIMINATING NUCLEAR WEAPONS COMPLETELY'

June 20, 1983, to a supporter of "Star Wars"

WITH REGARD TO A "Star Wars" defense system against nuclear weapons let me say the news media seems to be responsible for that descriptive term. Frankly I have no idea what the nature of such a defense might be. I simply asked our scientists to explore the possibility of developing such a defense. My thinking is that if such a defense can be found we could then move to get an agreement on eliminating nuclear weapons completely....

You and I are in agreement also about our dependence on God. Without His help there is no way we can be successful.

'NOT PURELY THEM VERSUS US'

Sept. 19, 1983, to a man in Los Angeles after a Soviet fighter jet shot down a South Korean civilian airliner

I CAN UNDERSTAND the frustration of those who want some kind of punishment imposed on the perpetrators of the Korean Airline massacre. No one is more frustrated than I am. Do you believe that I and my advisers from Secretaries of State and Defense, the Joint Chiefs of Staff and others in the National Security Council did not review every possibility? There were things that might have sounded good on the TV news but wouldn't have meant a thing in reality. Send their diplomatic people home? They would send ours home. And believe me this is no time for us to be without eyes and ears in Moscow....

In reality this is not purely them versus us. It is the Soviet Union against the world and we intend to keep it that way.

'THOSE MEN AREN'T FORGOTTEN'

Nov. 3, 1984, to a couple who lost a son in the bombing of the U.S. Marines barracks in Beirut

I KNOW THERE ARE no words that can lessen your pain. I wish there were. But believe me those men aren't forgotten—by me or by the American people. And nothing has angered me more than those who for political purposes have charged they were not serving a worthwhile cause. Our Marines and all of you deserve better than that.

Even now the possibility of a final peace in that tragic land exists only because of the presence of our Marines and their fellows in the multinational force during that year.... Only if we give up on trying to obtain peace will their sacrifice have been in vain. We will not do that.

'OUR PEOPLE LOOK TO US FOR LEADERSHIP'

Nov. 28, 1985, to Soviet General Secretary Mikhail Gorbachev on his hopes for nuclear-arms reductions

THE TRUTH IS THAT the United States has no intention of using its strategic defense program to gain any advantage, and there is no development underway to create space-based offensive weapons. Our goal is to eliminate any possibility of a first strike from either side. This being the case, we should be able to find a way, in practical terms, to relieve the concerns you have expressed....

And can't our negotiators deal more frankly and openly with the question of how to eliminate a first-strike potential on both sides? Your military now has an advantage in this area—a three to one advantage in warheads that can destroy hardened targets with little warning. That is obviously alarming to us, and explains perhaps many of the efforts we are making in our modernization program. You may feel perhaps that the United States has some advantages in other categories. If so, let's insist that our negotiators face up to these issues and find a way to improve the security of both countries by agreeing on appropriately balanced reductions. If you are as sincere as I am in not seeking to secure or preserve one-sided advantages, we will find a solution to these problems.... Both of us have advisers and assistants, but, you know, in the final analysis, the responsibility to preserve peace and increase cooperation is ours. Our people look to us for leadership, and nobody can provide it if we don't.

'AN ENTHUSIASTIC LAYING ON OF HANDS'

July 8, 1988, to former actor and U.S. senator from California George Murphy after Reagan's summit meeting in Moscow

YOU CAN'T BELIEVE how warm and friendly the ordinary people on the streets were. There was an enthusiastic laying on of hands, women were embracing Nancy and crying when she had to move on and there could be no doubt it was for real.

But that leads to something else; the people have of course heard of glasnost and evidently liked what they heard. Murphy for the first time, I believe there could perhaps one day be a stirring of the people that would make the bureaucrats pay attention.

'A WONDROUS JOURNEY'

Oct. 13, 1994, to former British prime minister Margaret Thatcher

ACROSS THE MILES I hope you'll feel the warm wishes and blessings we send on the occasion of your birthday. What a wonderful opportunity to celebrate you and your lifetime of accomplishments and tell you how much you have meant to us through the years.

How blessed I have been to celebrate so many of life's special moments with you.... It's been a wondrous journey, Margaret, and I pray that the coming years will be equally rewarding and joyful.

The Reagans (circa 1915; from left, Jack, Neil, Ronald and Nelle) moved four times before Ronald's fourth birthday.

Fresh out of college in 1932, Reagan landed a job as a radio sportscaster in Davenport, Iowa.

Twice-divorced Jane Wyman described herself as "a nightclub girl" before marrying Reagan in 1940.

Eager to flaunt the studio's new male ingenue, Warner Bros. featured Reagan in nine movies in 1938.

Though her marriage to Reagan was on shaky ground, Wyman insisted that they adopt Michael (with sister Maureen, circa 1946).

At a 1947 hearing before the House Un-American Activities Committee, SAG president Reagan denounced the Communist Party but defended its right to exist.

SAG members Reagan and (from left) Wyman, Henry Fonda, Boris Karloff and Gene Kelly voted in October 1946 to cross craft-union strike lines.

A lifelong fan of westerns, Reagan stomped out the bad guys as Marshal Frame Johnson in 1953's Law and Order.

Taking time off from his job as TV host for GE Theater, Reagan and second wife Nancy enjoy a night out at the Brown Derby in 1955.

During his eight years with GE, Reagan visited 139 plants, including this one in Schenectady, N.Y., in 1956.

Reagan's 1964 speech supporting GOP presidential hopeful Barry Goldwater ignited his run two years later for governor of California.

LET'S STOP THE HUMBUG LET'S NULLIFY BROWN BY VOTING REAGAN

STUDENT POWER S.D.S.

A student demonstration in Sacramento in 1967 targeted Governor Reagan and his proposed tuition plans and budget cuts.

Presidential
Roundtable

A FRESH TAKE ON THE REAGAN REVOLUTION

A PANEL MODERATED BY JON MEACHAM
WITH MICHAEL BESCHLOSS,
MICHAEL DUFFY AND CRAIG SHIRLEY

On the occasion of the 10th anniversary of the death of the 40th president, TIME *brought together four noted historians to discuss his life and legacy. On our panel were Michael Beschloss, author of nine books on the modern presidency and a contributing columnist for the* New York Times; *Michael Duffy, a* TIME *deputy managing editor and co-author of* The Presidents Club: Inside the World's Most Exclusive Fraternity; *and Craig Shirley, a Reagan biographer and the Visiting Reagan Scholar at Eureka College. Jon Meacham, a* TIME *contributing editor and the Pulitzer Prize–winning author of* American Lion: Andrew Jackson in the White House, *moderated the conversation.*

JON MEACHAM: Let's start with a counterfactual. How different do you think the world would be if Ronald Reagan had never been elected president?

CRAIG SHIRLEY: I think he completely changes the Republican Party. In many ways, as the late political analyst Samuel Lubell suggested, the Republican Party was the moon to the Democratic Party's sun. The Democratic Party, from 1932 up to the late 1970s, was the dominant political party. It was the party of hope. It was the party of fun. It was the party of optimism. The Republican Party was the green-eyeshade party, the party of "no," the party of "eat your spinach." And Reagan breaks apart the old New Deal coalition and creates a new political dynamic with a new Republican Party that is culturally, ideologically and philosophically different, far different, from the party of, say, Herbert Hoover or even of Dwight Eisenhower.

If Reagan was not elected, I suspect that in 1980 the Republican Party would have nominated George Bush, and he might well have beaten Carter, but he would have not created a political revolution. There was no revolutionary in the field in 1980 other than Ronald Reagan. And in so doing, he upends the political dialectic.

So, in short, had Reagan not been elected, the Republican Party and the Democratic Party probably would have stayed on the straight-line trajectory that they'd been on from 1932 until 1980.

MICHAEL DUFFY: I think Craig's right. It's hard to imagine 20th-century America turning out the way it did without Ronald Reagan. He steered the nation to the right after Lyndon Johnson's Great Society and, of course, after the Roosevelt era, and he did so in a way that hasn't really stopped.

We're still in a center-right nation. Our instincts still owe a lot to the man who burst on the scene in 1964 or 1966, depending on when you start. Years after his death, he amazingly still plays a fairly big role in, if not driving, certainly hovering over the political conversation in our country. And his impact was felt overseas as well.

So I think one of the amazing things about Reagan is just how big his influence was and how big it remains. That, I wouldn't have guessed a decade ago.

SHIRLEY: Let me just jump back in here. I don't want to be too effusive to start out with, but nobody in the Republican Party calls themselves a Nixon Republican or a Bush Republican, but everybody calls themselves a Reagan Republican.

MICHAEL BESCHLOSS: I would also say that had anyone but Ronald Reagan become president in 1981, the Cold War would not have ended when it did and on terms as favorable to the U.S. as they were.

MEACHAM: If you're ranking presidents in terms of the order of magnitude of their influence, where would you put Reagan, at least in the 20th century?

BESCHLOSS: It's hard to say that Reagan would be very far under the top. And I think the way you framed this is very good, Jon, which is that if you take Reagan out of the equation, and the president in the early '80s is Bush or Carter or anyone else who might have been president, the period since then would have been very different. Hard to think of many presidents during the 20th century where you would say that.

MEACHAM: Craig, biographically just take us back a bit. What was it in Reagan's life that prepared him, armed him, gave him the capacity to do the things that we've been describing?

SHIRLEY: Most men reach a point in their life in their 30s or 40s where they adopt a worldview, and that becomes their settled outlook for the rest of their lives. Reagan was unusual in that he was never static. People think of him as unchanging, but that wasn't the case. He was always dynamic, he was always evolving.

The Ronald Reagan of 1980 is vastly different from the Ronald Reagan of 1964 in his speech for Barry Goldwater. The Reagan of '64 is a garden-variety conservative, also an angry conservative. He's against the New Deal, he's against the Great Society and he's against Johnson, but he isn't really optimistic. The Reagan that we saw in 1980 is a much sunnier figure. He embraces a Jeffersonian and a Thomas Paine view of the world that puts the individual at the center of the universe.

Two of his favorite philosophers were Aleksandr Solzhenitsyn and Paine. And you say, well, how can that be? Here's Paine, the very flower of the Enlightenment, but Solzhenitsyn gives a speech at Harvard in 1978 eviscerating the Enlightenment. But Reagan was able to synthesize the two positions, and he coined a phrase that I think is significant. It was "man with God," not "man and God," but "man with God." He believed very much in the individual, but he also believed very much in the spiritual individual.

You see his evolution in thinking by the time he runs in 1980. He's still evolving. He adopts the tax cuts, he rejects détente and embraces a new approach toward the Soviets. Instead of being anti-abortion, he's pro-life. He's emphasizing the optimistic aspects of humanity and culture instead of just the anti–concentration of power in the state. And none of this is possible without Nancy Reagan.

BESCHLOSS: One of the toughest things to understand about a president is his degree of religious belief. While Reagan was serving, even people who were Reagan allies tended to feel that this was not a deeply religious person. Even after the assassination attempt he didn't go to church, and so forth. Yet on reflection I think Reagan was much more religious than many people understood in the 1980s. Truman is the only recent example, I think, who is like this—where the president turns out to be a lot more religious than he seemed at the time. It's usually so much the opposite.

Look at his childhood, which on paper was very insecure—the alcoholic father who was out of work, the mother who was hugely supportive. In retrospect, the more I learn about Reagan the more important I think his religious belief was in giving him the sense of optimism that Craig spoke of. Most people with that kind of a childhood would not be very optimistic or self-confident.

DUFFY: In terms of influences you find in his biography, I also think his early encounter with communism can't be overemphasized. In countering charges of communism as the SAG [Screen Actors Guild] president in the 1940s and 1950s, after being a New Deal Democrat, it challenges him in a way, both as a labor leader and as someone who had pretty good relations with the big studios. He begins moving to the right well ahead of the rest of the nation, after having been a Roosevelt supporter and having campaigned for and appeared with Truman.

SHIRLEY: And he supported 1940s actress and Democratic congresswoman Helen Gahagan Douglas.

DUFFY: It's a very long and interesting journey that in some ways helped him later as a presidential candidate and a leader because he could say, "Well, I used to be a Democrat." He was able to speak to the other party's strengths and its weaknesses. This gave him a much bigger, broader, deeper narrative than a lot of the candidates we see today who came up without looking one way or the other.

BESCHLOSS: His discovery and disillusionment over communism comes at the same time as two other things. Reagan before the war, I think you would agree, was a relatively innocent person to the extent that someone intelligent in Hollywood really would be. After the war his film career is over, at least compared to what it might have been before, and so is his marriage to Jane Wyman. So this is this very unhappy person who's gotten two primal surprises in his life. And another surprise, as we've said, is communism. So he becomes a deeper and more serious and more skeptical person.

SHIRLEY: I want to jump in on this ranking thing and defer to John Patrick Diggins, who I got to know well late in his life. He was in many ways the unofficial historian for the American left in the 20th century. He was a San Francisco State student and assistant professor in the 1960s and part of the free-speech movement, and actually did battle with Governor Reagan. He was very critical of Reagan until his last book, which was in 2007, about Reagan, called *Fate, Freedom and the Making of History.* This liberal historian comes to the conclusion that Reagan is one of our four greatest presidents alongside of Washington, Lincoln and Franklin Roosevelt, using the criterion that each man saved many lives. I think that that is a pretty worthy way to judge an American president.

DUFFY: I also will bring in Barack Obama to testify as my next witness to Reagan's clout so many years after his death. In some of his worst moments as president, Obama—and this isn't very widely known—has actually looked to Reagan's example and consulted his aides for inspiration in how to find the handle again and get back on top of his own game.

BESCHLOSS: Not to mention what Obama said in Reno in 2008— that he aspired to be a transformational president the way Reagan was. Which was not warmly received in all quarters of the Democratic Party.

DUFFY: Yes, especially by the Clintons.

MEACHAM: A lot of folks on the left might say that here we are talking about a president who had a propensity for misstatements, and who committed potentially impeachable offenses in Iran-contra. Yet even in real time many Americans gave Reagan a pass on questions that would have sunk lesser mortals. Why was that?

DUFFY: This is the hard essay question on the test.

SHIRLEY: Well, for one thing, Reagan in 1980 is not someone who just burst on the scene. Lincoln was only a national figure for essentially seven years; Reagan had been a national figure since the time he was in Hollywood. People forget how enormously popular *GE Theater* was. The Emmy Award–winning show enjoyed its highest rankings within months after Reagan took the helm as host in 1954. Of course there were his movies, and *Death Valley Days*. And then as governor. So he had a deep wellspring of affection among those Americans who had made a psychological investment in him before they invested their votes in him in the primaries of 1976 and 1980 or the general election of 1980.

When he leaves office in January of 1989 his approval rating overall is 68%, and his approval among African Americans is 40%. Unemployment is at 5.3%. Inflation plummeted. Interest rates are down to about 10%. The Cold War that we were arguably losing in 1980 we're now winning. The Berlin Wall is about to come down. He wasn't perfect, but he was leaving the country in much better shape than he found it.

Don't forget, too, that Reagan's mistakes had to be seen in context—and the context was pretty gloomy. We'd lost a president in 1963, we lost a war, gas prices were out of control, as were inflation and interest rates, we're losing a Cold War, we lost another president because of his corruption and contempt for the Constitution, we have the failed presidencies of Gerald Ford and Jimmy Carter and Lyndon Johnson. So he has that backdrop, that contrast to play off of.

DUFFY: I think this is really about missions defined and missions accomplished. He came in saying he wanted to fix the economy and put America back on top, and by late 1986, when the worst of Iran-contra begins to start, or early '87, he's done most of that and the public has reelected him by a vast, overwhelming margin that shocked many people. They just said, "You know, he's worth it."

MEACHAM: Every political party or political movement to some extent is shaped by the tension between purists within that movement and, for lack of a better term, pragmatists. More than any other modern political figure, with the possible exception of FDR, Reagan was basically able to control that dynamic. And when people talk about wanting to be a Reagan Republican, I think they're talking about the ideology rather than the pragmatism, the skills of the union president that he brought to the highest levels. So my question is, do you think there's room for a pragmatic Reagan figure in the Republican Party right now—a party that seems particularly riven by that tension between purists and pragmatists?

BESCHLOSS: To win the presidential nomination of the Republican Party now it would probably be great if you had another Reagan, but no one is saying that so-and-so is Ronald Reagan revisited. He was a pragmatist who posed as a purist. One of the most interesting things he ever said was that if I can get, what is it, 80% of what I want in a deal, that's perfectly fine for me. He had the skills. He was a natural. This was a bundle of skills that you're only going to find probably once every 100 years. And that is why it's so difficult for the Republicans to find someone like that now.

DUFFY: Right. In what political cycle, 2048, 2052, will we stop having primary debates at the Reagan library in order to somehow invoke the spirit of a man born in 1911?

BESCHLOSS: That's a sign that no one since then has caught on. If there is another hugely popular Republican two-term president, that is about the time it's going to happen. In fact, one metric of the current success of a political party is how recent their most popular role model is.

DUFFY: Exactly. The other thing that helped Reagan was that sunny disposition; Americans like that. Clinton had it. And of course Roosevelt had it. The man with the first-class temperament. It's sort of a killer app in politics. It helps you sustain the worst. Reagan had it like few others—and there aren't other figures on the scene now who have it. Probably for the reasons that Michael had said before: Reagan had come out of such a difficult situation and been raised by a mother who was nearly evangelical, and he knew how to look at the glass half full. And he taught the nation how to do that.

MEACHAM: Craig, of the people here, you have the most hands-on engagement in the political arena at the moment. How often do you have potential Republican candidates or officeholders asking you what would Reagan do?

SHIRLEY: Well, about every 30 minutes! That's an interesting question, because I get that often. Reaganism is misshapen by so many people on the right because they don't really understand the man and his core. Everybody here understands that the rhetoric was one thing, but the practice was another. He worked within a conservative framework, but it was a different kind of conservatism than he found with Goldwater. This was much more evocative of Jefferson and Paine, as I mentioned, more of a bottom-up conservatism than the top-down style in the days of the British statesman Edmund Burke.

That was a new way of looking at things. In 1981, pitching the tax cuts to a group of conservatives, Reagan talked about the tax cuts as being part of a larger framework about reordering man's relationship to the state. Now, A, that's a very profound thought. And B, there are very few politicians who talk like that anymore.

DUFFY: There's a particular anomaly about the spirit of Reagan, or the ghost of Reagan, 25 years after he left office that makes him harder and harder to invoke. He leaves office in 1989 and, compared to most former presidents, he just goes dark. He tells the nation within just a few years that he has Alzheimer's. He does not engage in a 25-year redemption campaign or whitewashing campaign that so many of our modern presidents have had a chance to do. In a very short period of time he simply is no more. So he doesn't leave us with the sort of long finish that certainly Bill Clinton is going to enjoy and George W. Bush can have anytime he wants. Obama's is yet to begin, but it could go 30-some years.

SHIRLEY: Eisenhower went back to Gettysburg and never obsessed about his presidency or his role in history. Jefferson went back to Monticello and didn't obsess about it. The very last line in the Reagan diary is, "Then home and start of our new life." And he closes the diary. It's utterly remarkable that a 77-year-old man would have that outlook.

BESCHLOSS: The last line of Eisenhower's memoirs was something like, "And so Mamie and I went back to Gettysburg where we expected to spend the rest of our lives," period. I always wondered when I read that whether Reagan had at some level remembered that.

MEACHAM: Duffy, you wrote a book about relationships between incumbents and former presidents, as well as formers and formers. What did Reagan learn from the presidents he had known?

DUFFY: I'd love to start with Eisenhower, because my favorite early Reagan story is the quiet support Eisenhower in 1966 gave this young former actor who's running for governor of California—pointers that say, "Keep it light, keep it bright, keep it positive." Answer the question about the John Birch Society this way. Answer the charge of anti-Semitism, which was spurious, this way. He's tutoring this guy in whom he sees some promise at the same time that his own vice president, Richard Nixon, is preparing to run for the presidential nomination in '68. Probably before Ronald Reagan imagined being president—or maybe not—he has a pretty good tutor in Ike.

BESCHLOSS: It shows a lot about Reagan that Eisenhower, whom you would expect to be skeptical of someone who was an actor and who did not have a particularly active role in World War II, and who had so little management experience, got it and saw this potential in Reagan.

DUFFY: Reagan and Nixon dance around each other. Two men, two conservatives, two Southern Californians, in effect dance around each other for the better part of a generation, neither really helping the other much. Different kinds of Republicans, almost from two different ages, although the first and the second were reversed in age.

BESCHLOSS: And Nixon had such contempt for him.

DUFFY: Right. Thought he just couldn't be taken seriously. Nixon really had the actor problem with Reagan.

BESCHLOSS: I think until the end of his life Nixon could still not understand what happened.

DUFFY: He in confidence told John Ehrlichman and Bob Haldeman that he thought Reagan was odd.

MEACHAM: Well, he knew odd.

DUFFY: This was at a time when Nixon was running the air-conditioning and burning logs in the fireplace at the same time. And, of course, Reagan runs against Ford and Ford beats him, but he weakened Ford in the process and Ford never forgave him. Reagan doesn't have any use for Carter. So if you have to give a first position to somebody, you might give it to Ike. He had very little coaching except from Ike.

SHIRLEY: Frankly, Richard Nixon was intimidated by Reagan. Reagan is a Hollywood actor and a pretty good athlete and had been successful. Here's Nixon, who was not a good athlete, kind of homely. And I think also Nixon was always jealous of Reagan's superior speaking ability. That was clear.

BESCHLOSS: I think both Nixon and Reagan felt that if Reagan had made a full-out effort to win the nomination in 1968 he might have gotten it.

SHIRLEY: Here's how close Reagan came in 1968. First of all, to Reagan's ambitions: in 1966, one week after he was elected governor, he convened a meeting in his house to discuss running for president in 1968. At the convention in '68, if Clarke Reed, the national committeeman from Mississippi and Mr. South, can be flipped from Nixon to Reagan, and if Florida and another state can be flipped, Reagan would have been the nominee in 1968. Nixon is nominated in Miami Beach only when they get alphabetically to Wisconsin in the roll call. Nixon receives 200 fewer delegate votes in '68 than Goldwater did in '64. His nomination was extremely tenuous.

BESCHLOSS: Also, what if Reagan had gone to Strom Thurmond early in '68 and said, "I'm going to do this seriously and I want you to support me." Rather than Thurmond supporting Nixon, he supports Reagan and then Reagan might have won.

SHIRLEY: Thurmond told him, "Young man, you're going to be president someday, but not this time." Once Nixon gets that nomination there's a little push on Nixon to make Reagan the future of the Republican Party, his running mate, and Nixon just wouldn't have any of it.

BESCHLOSS: The Republicans in '68 and '72 were really more a Reagan party than a Nixon party. I wouldn't overplay this, but that would lead Nixon to think of himself to some extent as governing at Reagan's sufferance. At the same time, as he has obviously unwarranted contempt for Reagan intellectually, Nixon talks to Reagan in the most condescending tones.

MEACHAM: Let me ask, to what extent do you all agree with the following piece of what George W. Bush would call the common wisdom, that his father's election in '88 was, at least in the casting of the votes, a third term for Reagan?

BESCHLOSS: Sure. Well, the Van Buren rule [in which no vice president since Martin Van Buren in 1836 had been directly elected to succeed his incumbent president] had been proved wrong.

SHIRLEY: There was a *New York Times* poll shortly after that election that essentially showed that the people who voted for Bush thought they were voting for a third term for Ronald Reagan.

DUFFY: As Craig said at the start, Reagan had rewritten the coalitions in '80 and '84, and Bush was smart enough to temper his message to make it kinder and gentler, and to win over enough of the people who had had enough of that to hold the coalition together for at least another year or two. It didn't last much longer than that. But he was able to run on Reagan's back, get elected by a comfortable margin.

MEACHAM: Do you all think there are people out there, governors maybe, doing the kind of relentless homework, doing the kind of thinking and rubber-chicken-ing that they might plausibly emerge as Reagan-like figures? Or has the culture shifted in a way that if you are an aspiring president, you're so consumed with the minute-to-minute that you can't build that kind of base over time and win the third time you run?

DUFFY: I would say I hope there's someone out there doing it. I really hope so, of some party, because we could use a transformational figure of Reagan's size and scope now. I don't really care what party he or she is from, but I do think we need someone who can shake up these ossified lines and coalitions, because both parties have stopped trying to do things differently or have anything like the clarity of vision or the focus that Reagan had.

SHIRLEY: The answer is that I don't think so, but the truth is I don't know and none of us knows. And I think it bears remembering that Ronald Reagan wasn't Ronald Reagan before Ronald Reagan was Ronald Reagan.

In the 1970s, in '76 and in 1980, the Republican establishment despised this guy. They loathed him. The Washington Republicans thought he was a grade-B actor with premature orange hair and that he was a lightweight. They thought he was the George Wallace of the Republican Party. There was a great fear. Of course, the American left thought even less of him, if possible. It was just the American people had a different opinion than the elites of either party did. And when he came into the presidency, there were not a lot of high hopes that he was going to be successful or become a two-term president.

That said, projecting forward I don't see very many people in the Republican Party who actually think deeply about things in the way Reagan did. But for the sake of the country, let's hope so; let's hope there are men and women on both sides who are thinking about things.

BESCHLOSS: Yes, and the case of Reagan should give everyone hope, since so many people never saw the depths and the potential of the man in real time in a way that we do now in history.

MEACHAM: Let's end on this: What do you think the Reagan legacy is in sum here on the 10th anniversary of his death?

BESCHLOSS: I think he would probably end by saying, "It wasn't me." He'd say it was the people who were alongside of him trying to make things the way that they should be.

SHIRLEY: I want to disagree slightly. I'm working on a book now about the post-presidency, and I came across a very, very wise comment from Lou Cannon in which he said that Reagan worked at being underestimated. In other words, it wasn't organic. It didn't come naturally. He worked at it. And he was able to use that in the campaigns and as president. But his last speech, his farewell, he puts his chest out. He's pretty proud of what he's done. This is a man who …

BESCHLOSS: But remember, it's all about accomplishments, not about himself.

SHIRLEY: Yes, but it was about his accomplishments …

BESCHLOSS: I guess what I'm saying is in contrast to certain other current figures, it was always "we" and not "I."

SHIRLEY: Well, that was part of his Catholic perspective. His father was Catholic, and so he had a parish perspective. He rarely said "I," "me" or "my." He preferred the pronouns "we," "us" and "ours."

DUFFY: It'll be fascinating to know how Reagan is viewed 10 years from now. While Reagan disappeared rather quickly from public view after he left the presidency, the rather vast Reagan white-washing and mythmaking machine has not stopped. I think there are more books about Reagan than any other president of the 20th century, by a long distance. He revitalized the nation economically and strategically overseas. In terms of his political impact he really started the conversation that the welfare state had become too big. He didn't shrink it much himself, but he did set the wheels in motion that would begin to limit its growth. As he might say, "Not bad—not bad at all."

The GOP Icon

WHY THE TEA PARTY FORGIVES HIS SINS

BY ALEX ALTMAN

Alex Altman is a Washington correspondent for TIME.

W HEN DAVID KNITTLE DECIDED TO FORM a local Tea Party group in 2009, he knew exactly what to call it. Like many conservatives, he describes himself as a Reagan Republican. "Ronald Reagan represents to me all that is great about America," he says. To Knittle, a Los Angeles–area health-care worker in his mid-50s, the Tea Party embodied the same set of values that Reagan espoused: sound economic policy, lower taxes, smaller government and more individual freedom. And so he dubbed the group Reagan's Regiments—a title coined by Reagan himself, who bequeathed it to his army of supporters in his 1989 farewell address.

The homage was hardly surprising. Ten years after his death, Ronald Reagan remains the closest thing the Republican Party has to a secular saint. As the GOP struggles to chart a course back to the White House, Reagan is its lodestar, one of the few leaders on whose greatness the party's fractious factions can agree. That view is shared in the Tea Party movement, a constellation of grassroots organizations that tend to regard most elected Republicans as only marginally better than Democrats. When the movement began brewing in 2009, Reagan's name, image and famous adages about the evils of big government became as ubiquitous at Tea Party rallies as tricorn hats and Gadsden flags.

"He was the Tea Party of his time," Michael Reagan, one of the president's sons, declared in 2010. "He would have been at the forefront of the Tea Party movement, urging it on and devoting every last ounce of his energy to its progress in restoring America."

Perhaps, but if Reagan were to take the measure of the Tea Party in 2014, he might conceivably turn and flee. Conversely, the Tea Party's continuing idolatry of Reagan is somewhat curious. At one time or another, the 40th president smashed nearly every commandment the conservative movement regards as sacred. A closer look at Reagan's time in office would suggest that he is a less than ideal fit for a sometimes rigid political movement that is willing to allow the government to shut down when its demands aren't met.

Consider Reagan's record on what the Tea Party holds most dear. He proposed the largest tax hike by any governor in the history of the United States. As president, he raised taxes 11 times, never submitted a balanced-budget request, hiked the debt ceiling 18 times and bemoaned the congressional brinkmanship that "consistently brings the government to the edge of default before facing its responsibility." Plus, the federal deficit nearly tripled.

The apostasies aren't just fiscal. Reagan was a onetime union leader who extolled the virtues of collective bargaining. As governor of California, he championed environmental legislation and signed a bill making it easier to get an abortion. The only U.S. president to divorce, he incensed the Christian right by nominating a socially moderate judge, the future swing vote Sandra Day O'Connor, to serve on the Supreme Court. He cut sweeping deals with liberal legislators like Tip O'Neill, the Democratic speaker of the House. He signed a major overhaul of the U.S. immigration system that ultimately granted amnesty to some 3 million undocumented immigrants.

All these moves are anathema to the Tea Party movement. "There's a kind of delusional quality in the Tea Party's affinity for Reagan," says Matthew Dallek, author of the 2000 book *The Right Moment: Ronald Reagan's First Victory and the Decisive Turning Point in American Politics*. "Certainly Reagan governed in a way that the Tea Party, to the extent they're true to their beliefs, would probably find abhorrent."

Even some Tea Party members who came of age under Reagan and consider him a great president are puzzled by the way he's worshipped. "There's an irony in the idolization of Reagan," admits Ned Ryun, a conservative strategist and the president of American Majority, a group that trains Tea Party activists how to run for local office. "He would be considered today a very, very soft conservative—if not a moderate."

That's a far cry from Reagan's reputation during his rise to power, when he was regarded by many as an archconservative ideologue. But the party has lurched rightward during Barack Obama's presidency. Today, in a modern Republican nominating contest dominated by activists who prize purity and punish compromise, Reagan's record might work against him. One marker of the GOP's evolution came during a Republican presidential debate in 2011, when the eight candidates arrayed onstage were asked whether they would accept a deal of $10 in spending cuts for every dollar of tax increases. Each vowed to turn it down. The crowd erupted in applause.

So why does the Tea Party venerate Reagan, who violated so many of its values? Part of it, say Tea Party activists, was his matchless ability to market conservatism to the masses. He was an unabashed believer in the tenets of American exceptionalism, individual initiative and the free market—and enumerated their merits with the fervor of the converted. Nor, supporters say, would he back away from his beliefs. After Barry Goldwater's drubbing in 1964, most political observers pronounced conservatism dead. Reagan built a coalition out of its ashes.

"That's the kind of stuff that makes Reagan such an icon for the Tea Party movement," says Jeff Reynolds, a Republican political consultant and chairman of the Portland-based Oregon Tea Party. "He talked passionately and eloquently about conservatism and the values that make America great. If you're looking for somebody who espouses the conservative ideal and articulates why more government is a bad thing, there's virtually nobody better."

Reagan is admired for many qualities, one of which is simply that the public loves a winner, and he piled up plenty of impressive, and even historic, victories. In 1980 and 1984, he authored two electoral blowouts. He is also credited with winning the Cold

War, the epic struggle of the second half of the 20th century, without firing a shot. At a moment of dwindling national morale, he toppled a seemingly ascendant communist threat.

"President Reagan understood that weakness is an invitation to war," says Republican senator Ted Cruz. The Texan, part of a new generation of Tea Party icons, might find fault with some of Reagan's domestic accomplishments, but he says he patterns his own foreign policy after the 40th president's "peace through strength" credo. "The surest way to avoid war is to be strong enough to defend yourself," Cruz says. "And by rebuilding our defense and speaking the truth, Reagan accomplished, in concert with Margaret Thatcher and Pope John Paul II, the most extraordinary victory for peace in centuries."

During the early phases of his career, the Republican establishment derided Reagan as a dangerous extremist. A former actor from outside the party's clubby confines, he was widely viewed as inexperienced. In 1976 he had the temerity to challenge a sitting president from his own party, running to the right of incumbent Gerald Ford. He lost, but in the process proved that the country had a taste for his flavor of conservatism. And there is no question that the Tea Party sees in Reagan's career a narrative arc it would like to repeat. "Members of the Tea Party would love to see themselves as rebels who are reviled by the mainstream," says Dallek, the historian, "but who herald the American future."

Tea Partyers who take a textured view of Reagan's shortcomings are willing to give him a pass. They note that his deficit spending came during the military buildup of the Cold War, and at a time when the national debt was smaller; that his tax hikes were offset by cuts; that compromise is a necessary part of divided government. "You don't get everything you want as a president," says Knittle, the founder of Reagan's Regiments.

"His record is not as conservative as it could have been, and there are certainly issues on which we disagree," says Reynolds.

"But you always want to look at the big picture instead of nitpicking over issues. Reagan wasn't afraid to be conservative on the stump. He didn't moderate his views. He didn't sell out his ideals. He found a way to express conservative principles in a way that won people over."

And that includes members of the Tea Party, who have demonstrated that they hold those who refuse to sell out in the highest regard and will likely remain loyal to Reagan's memory—at least until a more strident conservative ascends to the White House.

The Private Man

MOST AT HOME WITH HIS THOUGHTS—AND NANCY

BY MOLLY MOORE

Molly Moore is a former national and foreign correspondent for the Washington Post *and author of* A Woman at War, *her personal account of the first Gulf War.*

HE IS LARGELY REMEMBERED AS A VERY PUBLIC man. Indeed, one could reasonably argue that there are no professions more public than movie star and leader of the free world. And he is the sole individual ever to hold both titles.

During his years in the spotlight, Ronald Reagan seemed to embody the quintessential soft-spoken small-town boy who proved that one really could rise from modest beginnings to hold the highest seat in the realm. He was the handsome movie star who was never in danger of winning an Oscar himself but who nonetheless rubbed elbows with the likes of Bogie, Barbara Stanwyck and even Monroe. Details of his love life with actresses Jane Wyman and Nancy Davis were regular fare in the fan mags of the time. And in the golden early years of television, he entered millions of living rooms on Sunday evenings as the earnest host of *General Electric Theater*.

All that was before he became truly famous, when he became governor of a state so vast that its economy is ranked seventh largest in the world. Then, of course, president—voted in not by squeakers but by historic margins.

But that was his public face. In private, his was a much different story. Those who knew him didn't describe a blustery Oz ruling from on high. They described a man who found comfort behind the curtain, a man with few very close friends, even fewer deep relationships, and a greater fondness for the quiet companionship of a fine horse than for that of a chirpy starlet or gruff world leader. Above all he coveted his private space, where only the love of his life, Nancy, was truly welcome.

Reagan's keen desire to protect his private time even while president was captured in a story told by Michael Deaver, Reagan's longtime aide and friend. But even Deaver, now deceased, recalled in his 2001 book *A Different Drummer* being taken aback when he phoned his boss, then on his ranch, in 1983 shortly after a Soviet

Su-15 fighter shot down a commercial South Korean airliner, killing all 269 people on board, including 61 Americans. When Deaver told him he should return to Washington to deal with the crisis, Reagan responded, "Dammit, I'm the president whether I'm in California or the Oval Office."

"I'm sorry," Deaver responded, "but the American people expect their leader to be in Washington in times of crisis. It's just the way it is."

"Well, it's a stupid idea if you ask me," was the response.

To his credit, Reagan did return to Washington, eloquently denounced the Soviets, and rejected a growing consensus among his top advisers to consider sanctions or other penalties against the U.S.S.R. His instincts proved true, and rather than shift the story to the United States with what would effectively have been saber rattling, his decision kept the world's focus on the Soviet Union, and nations worldwide issued blistering denunciations. He also avoided a possible confrontation with the Soviets that might have slowed his designs to negotiate with them on larger issues.

MODEST BEGINNINGS FOR A QUIET CHILD

THE ROOTS OF REAGAN'S YEN FOR PERSONAL SPACE and his difficulty in forging lasting relationships can be found, not surprisingly, in his youth. Looking back on his Midwestern American upbringing, he freely—and strategically in letters and political speeches—acknowledged that he was intimately familiar with the challenges of poverty. But he was more likely to describe his childhood as a series of "rare Huck Finn–Tom Sawyer idylls." By his telling, he went skinny-dipping in farm ponds in summer and skated on frozen rivers in winter. His mother sparked his interest in acting with her work in local theater. And his father inspired him to believe in the great American dream through his relentless pursuit of the next big job.

The true portrait was a great deal less Rockwellian. His father,

John Edward "Jack" Reagan, was an alcoholic who dragged the family from town to town in search of work, usually as a salesman with grand ideas that were repeatedly dashed by his passion for drink, his poor business acumen or the genuine hard luck of a faltering economy.

Neil, Ronald's older brother, recalled one period when his mother or father would hand him a dime to buy a soup bone at the butcher shop. The dime came with the reminder for 6-year-old Neil "to ask the butcher for liver for the cat." The Reagans had no cat. The family fried the liver for Sunday dinner. Ronald—known as "Dutch" because of his square-cut bangs—was just 3 at the time.

Ronald Wilson Reagan, the grandson of Irish immigrants, was born on Feb. 6, 1911, in the northwestern Illinois town of Tampico, population 820. The family lived for a while in a five-room flat above the Pitney general store where Reagan's father worked. His mother, Nelle Wilson Reagan, was a devout convert to the First Christian Church and an outspoken community activist.

When Ronald was 3, the family left Tampico for Chicago. At 4 he lived in Galesburg, at 7 in Monmouth, at 8 it was back to Tampico, and at 9 he and his family moved to Dixon, where they would live in five different rentals before Ronald bought Jack and Nelle their first home, in Los Angeles, in 1937. The family's itinerant lifestyle, say family members and historians, made it tough for Reagan to make or keep close friends throughout his life. "Moving so often during his formative years was difficult for Ronald Reagan," according to the official Ronald Reagan Presidential Foundation and Library biography. "He became a bit introverted and was shy about making deep friendships. He would read, draw and explore his surroundings, but had a reluctance to get too close to people that he might have to say goodbye to soon."

He was a quiet child, concluded Neil, "not one you would suspect would wind up an actor or a politician."

Reagan was conflicted even in his relationship with his father.

In his autobiography, *Where's the Rest of Me?*, he recounted: "I was 11 years old the first time I came home to find my father flat on his back on the front porch and no one there to lend a hand but me. He was drunk, dead to the world. I bent over him, smelling the sharp odor of whisky from the speakeasy. I got a fistful of his overcoat. Opening the door, I managed to drag him inside and get him to bed."

But he tempered that memory—as he did with many of the difficult moments of his life—adding, "In a few days he was the bluff, hearty man I knew and loved and will always remember."

Reagan's mother, who doted on her younger son, held the family together with her stoic outlook, strong will and devotion to the church. "My mother, bless her soul, told my brother and me from the time we were little, to understand this was a sickness and we weren't to hold it as a grudge, no matter what hardships it brought," Reagan wrote of his father's alcoholism.

Nelle Reagan had her own ways of expressing her frustration, however. While Jack was defying Prohibition, she wrote temperance plays that she performed at the church. One featured a little girl plaintively telling her father, "I love you, Daddy, except when you have that old bottle."

Challenges faced Ronald outside the family as well. Though he would sprout to 6 feet 1 later on, Dutch Reagan was small for his age and so nearsighted he couldn't see to catch a ball. As a result, he was often the last boy to be picked for sports teams. He couldn't read the blackboard in class, even when he sat in the front row. His parents bought him horn-rimmed glasses, but he despised them and often refused to wear them.

Young Ronald found solace roaming the woods and exploring nature, a pastime he would enjoy his entire life. He liked to draw and doodle—so much so that he once considered becoming a cartoonist. He loved to read adventure stories in books he checked out at the town library, where he was a regular visitor.

The shining light of Reagan's youth was his mother. In his autobiography, he wrote that she "had the conviction everyone loved her just because she loved them." His father's cynicism about the world never rubbed off on her, according to Reagan. Even in the toughest economic times, he wrote, she was quick to invite those less fortunate into the family's home, including the ex-convicts she worked with in a local rehabilitation program.

Reagan credited his mother with fostering his interest in acting by putting him onstage in her church plays, where he developed a taste for the spotlight and applause.

Dutch started high school with little fondness for schoolwork, but he quickly began to hone the lifelong skills that would serve him well. His near-photographic memory helped him maintain passable grades with minimal study, and his determination, spunk and upbeat attitude as a lineman on the football team endeared him to teammates, who eventually voted him captain.

His interest in acting blossomed in high school. He was cast in the lead male role in the school's production of Philip Barry's *You and I*—and won the heart of the female lead, Margaret "Mugs" Cleaver, a preacher's daughter and one of the most popular girls in school. At the end of high school, the caption under his yearbook picture read, "Life is just one grand sweet song, so start the music."

EMERGING INTO THE SPOTLIGHT

REAGAN AND CLEAVER SET OFF TOGETHER for Eureka College, a small Christian school about 100 miles from Dixon in Eureka, Ill. He supplemented his partial scholarship by washing dishes at a fraternity house and working as a lifeguard in Dixon (for which his pay rose over seven summers to $20 a week). A local newspaper story credited him with saving 77 people from drowning during his lifeguarding career.

Reagan followed much the same path in college as he had in high school, participating in drama, playing football and using his memorization skills to stay afloat in the classroom. "I know Ronald never opens a book," one of his economics professors lamented. "But he writes a good test."

After graduation, Reagan found work as a radio announcer, the job that would eventually lead him to Hollywood. But that time also marked his first heartbreak. He and Cleaver had dated for seven years; at graduation from Eureka in 1932 they held ivy strands around them, a school tradition that usually meant the couple would marry. Reagan would later write, "Our love and wholesome relationship did not survive growing up." He had focused his energy on his radio career, but he was still surprised in 1934 when Cleaver wrote him a letter from France, enclosing his engagement ring and telling him she was in love with another man.

In 1938 Reagan's romantic history repeated itself. Starring in the movie *Brother Rat*, he played a military-school cadet who wooed the commandant's daughter. The love interest was played by Jane Wyman, who reversed the roles offscreen and pursued Reagan as her own love interest. In stereotypical Hollywood style, their engagement was announced in an interview with a gossip columnist, and the couple wed on Jan. 26, 1940. Hollywood magazines promoted the two stars as the ideal Hollywood pair, especially after the birth of their daughter, Maureen, in 1941. Four years later they adopted a son, Michael.

World War II disrupted Reagan's acting career, though his poor eyesight kept him off the battlefield. Instead he made training and propaganda films for the Army's First Motion Picture Unit.

After military service, his marriage began disintegrating, frayed by the ambitions of both partners—Reagan with his time-consuming presidency of the Screen Actors Guild (SAG), Wyman with her all-engrossing acting career. They divorced in June 1948. In the court papers Wyman said Reagan spent too much time on SAG and not enough on her. He revealed his own emotional naiveté, saying of the split, "I suppose there had been warning signs, if only I hadn't been too busy, but small-town boys grow up thinking only other people get divorced. The plain truth was that such a thing was so far from ever being imagined by me that I had no resources to call on." To this day, Reagan is still the only U.S. president to have been divorced.

In November 1949 he met Nancy Davis when she approached him as president of SAG to have her name removed from the Hollywood blacklist of possible communist sympathizers during the McCarthy era. There was a Nancy Davis on the list, but it was someone else and it was making it hard for her to land parts.

His two previous relationships having ended badly, it was at first a hesitant romance. But in time Nancy, daughter of a wealthy Chicago surgeon, would become the one individual other than his mother whom he trusted and adored without hesitation or compromise. Then and later, while Reagan's colleagues would work into the wee hours or congregate at the local bar, he was most content heading out of the office at a reasonable hour to meet Nancy—just to enjoy a pleasant supper, maybe some popcorn, some quiet and a movie.

On March 4, 1952, Reagan married Davis, with actor William Holden as his best man. Seven months later daughter Patti was born, followed by a son, Ronald, in 1958.

Not long after Ronald and Nancy starred together in 1957's *Hellcats of the Navy*, she gave up acting to raise their children and support her husband's career. The two grew to become "not just husband and wife, but always the very best of friends," Reagan's older daughter, Maureen, later wrote.

ILL AT EASE WITH HIS CHILDREN

AS REAGAN TRANSFORMED HIS ACTING career into a political career, what he lacked as a deep thinker he made up for with an extraordinary ability to read human nature. He won over the prickliest leaders, whether in the California statehouse or the United Nations.

He also had an uncanny knack for putting people at ease—from foreign presidents to supporters who turned out at rope lines on the campaign trail. In his speeches he evinced a friendly, folksy empathy that often made him seem more like a deeply concerned uncle than a politician. Reagan the private man, however, could seem distant to those who were closest to him. "I always felt for a long time that there was a kind of veil between him and the rest of the world," said his press secretary Lyn Nofziger. "You could never really get in next to him." Nowhere was that more surprisingly evident than in his relationship with his own children, who provided some of the most personally troubling moments of his presidency. All four of them aired the family's dirty laundry in published memoirs.

Maureen, his eldest child, delivered a ruthless picture of a child raised by nannies and maids—all but ignored by parents who missed her school plays and even her high-school graduation. She said her father refused to return her telephone calls for eight years.

Michael, the son adopted as an infant by Reagan and Jane Wyman, wrote in his tell-all that his father "can give his heart to the country, but he just finds it difficult to hug his own children." Michael wrote that the standard family Thanksgiving invitation was "Come at 5 and be gone by 7."

White House spokesman Larry Speakes corroborated their assessments in his memoir, *Speaking Out*, noting, "There always seemed to be a controversy about when the Reagans had last seen the kids ... and who was coming for the holidays, if anybody. But where you really ran into a problem was when there was some serious presidential illness. This is the father of these four children, but most of the time the children didn't call to see how he was, and he and Mrs. Reagan didn't call them. It was very strange."

Reagan did seem to have flashes of self-recognition over his failures as a father. "I used to run around the offices when I'd found out that some of the staff of mine were staying in the office till 8 o'clock at night," he wrote. "I'd go in and curse them out and tell them they had families; go home to their families. But I went home with a full briefcase."

Throughout his life, Reagan was a prolific letter writer, but he never mailed what was perhaps one of his most heartfelt letters, one Patti says her mother found while cleaning out his drawers. He apparently started the letter when he heard that Patti was preparing to publish a book about her estrangement from her parents. He pleaded with her to soften the tone of the book and ended plaintively, "Please Patti, don't take away our memories of a daughter we truly love and whom we miss."

Reagan apparently worked on the letter over a period of more than a year because "he crossed out his age and increased his age by a year," Patti told television interviewer Katie Couric.

But his children also recounted some of their father's lighthearted moments in their books. Michael and his wife attended one of the nine inaugural balls hosted the night his father was sworn in for his first term in the White House. The new president straightened his white tie, and "all of a sudden he turned to us and, with a wink, jumped straight up in the air and clicked his heels. 'I'm the president of the United States.'"

HIS ULTIMATE REFUGE

IN THE WHITE HOUSE, REAGAN'S TWO most publicized personal quirks were his affinity for jelly beans—a taste he picked up while trying to kick a nasty pipe-smoking habit as governor of California—and his and Nancy's embrace of astrology in guiding the course of their daily lives. But even in the glare of the presidential spotlight, he coveted his quiet time with Nancy. One of the most iconic images of his private moments in the White House was a photograph of Reagan and the first lady eating their dinner off TV trays as they watched television, the president's favorite mode of unwinding after a day in the Oval Office.

Nothing quite evidenced Reagan's quest for bucolic solitude more than his ranch—or actually ranches. He had a few, the first an eight-acre spread he bought in 1945 in Northridge, a now bustling suburb of Los Angeles that was then an open pasture. Six years later, he purchased 250 acres in the Santa Monica Mountains.

But both properties paled in comparison with what would become Reagan's greatest refuge: his beloved 688-acre Rancho del Cielo (Ranch in the Sky) overlooking the Pacific Ocean and Santa Ynez Valley in Santa Barbara, Calif. He and Nancy acquired the ranch, featuring a homey white adobe with a red-tile roof, in his last year as governor of California. Reagan frequently said it was where he and Nancy were most at peace. In fact, he spent almost a year—335 days—of his eight-year presidency at the ranch. He relaxed by horseback riding, chopping brush and building fences.

John R. Barletta, part of Reagan's Secret Service detail, described agents' first encounter with the president-elect and his horses at the ranch in his book, *Riding with Reagan*.

"No one had any idea how to tie a horse, the president-elect ended up saddling the horses for the agents. Things only got worse once they started riding. President Reagan would ride fast and jump fences. He was really an English equestrian rider. The agents assigned to him did not know how to ride, and they were having trouble keeping up with him. One day, an agent fell off his horse and broke his arm. The president-elect dismounted his horse to take care of the agent.... The president was not supposed to be giving us aid and comfort. That was what we should be doing for him."

Reagan's favorite steed was El-Alamein, a spirited white Arabian that was a present from former Mexican president José López Portillo. Reagan was particularly fond of sneaking him jelly beans.

At 9 a.m. each day on the ranch, Reagan would ring an old bell hanging near the tack barn, signaling Nancy it was time for their daily ride. Though Nancy was never particularly fond of riding, she took it up because it was her husband's passion.

Jan. 20, 1989, was Ronald Reagan's last day as president of the United States. The final entry in his presidential diary, a document that is more a terse datebook than a compilation of introspective thought, reflected virtually no emotion. "Up fairly early. A little before 10 a.m. I went over to the Oval O. now looking pretty bare. Took a picture with the photo pool. Then I took a look at the desk for their photos and walked out the door."

Unlike many presidents who use their later years to try to burnish their legacies, Reagan largely disappeared from view. Not a surprise to those who knew him. But in November 1994, almost six years after leaving the White House, he emerged with a letter that shocked and saddened even those who once opposed him:

"My fellow Americans, I have recently been told that I am one of the millions of Americans who will be afflicted with Alzheimer's disease.... I now begin the journey that will lead me to the sunset of my life.... I only wish there was some way I could spare Nancy from this painful experience."

The disease prompted reconciliation between him and his children. When he became unable to travel to his ranch, Reagan rested in his 7,200-square-foot, three-bedroom, six-bath house with a heated swimming pool in Los Angeles's tony Bel-Air neighborhood. In the last years of his life, Nancy described her husband as being "in a distant place where I can no longer reach him."

Reagan died of complications of the disease on June 5, 2004, at his home, surrounded by Nancy and his children. He was 93 years old. His body is buried on the grounds of the Reagan presidential library in Simi Valley, Calif., beneath a gray granite wall with the inscription:

I KNOW IN MY HEART THAT MAN IS GOOD, THAT WHAT
IS RIGHT WILL ALWAYS EVENTUALLY TRIUMPH, AND THERE
IS PURPOSE AND WORTH TO EACH AND EVERY LIFE

Nancy Recalls Their Private Life Together

Nancy Reagan famously said, "My life really began when I met Ronald Reagan." When Alzheimer's started to take its toll on her husband, she found solace rereading the letters he had written her over the years. Judging by those letters, and her memories, captured in her book I Love You, Ronnie, *one might conclude that Reagan's life also began when he met his one true love.*

DATING IN HOLLYWOOD

LIKE ALL OTHER DATING PEOPLE IN HOLLYWOOD in those days, we spent time at first going out to nightclubs like Ciro's and Macombo and LaRue's, but neither of us was really crazy about nightlife. The glamour was fun, but we preferred to be with good friends or to be at my apartment on Hilgard Avenue in Westwood, having dinner, watching television, and popping popcorn.

LEARNING TO RIDE A HORSE

BEFORE LONG, RONNIE TAUGHT ME TO RIDE HORSES. ("Show him who's boss," he said to me the first time I got up on a horse. That's ridiculous, I thought. This animal knows perfectly well who's boss and it isn't me.) I took some spills—one, I remember, landed me right on my bottom—and I never became a great rider. But Ronnie rode, so I did too. I was, I suppose, a woman of the old school: If you wanted to make your life with a man, you took on whatever his interests were and they became your interests, too.

'MOMMIE POO' AND 'DADDIE POO'

RONNIE HAD STARTED CALLING ME MOMMIE when Patti was born. When I called her Patti Poo, he called me Mommie Poo. That led, somehow, to Mommie Poo Pants. Then to Daddie Poo Pants. The nicknames made us laugh—and becoming "Mommie" and "Daddie" also meant that our lives were changing, in very real ways. We were parents now—but we were also careful to never forget our marriage. We were always vigilant to not be "careless," as Ronnie put it in one letter, "with the treasure that is ours—namely what we are to each other."

REAGAN, THE COMPETITOR

YEARS LATER, PEOPLE WOULD SOMETIMES SAY I pushed Ronnie into a career in politics. Nothing could be further from the truth, and saying that shows a real misunderstanding of Ronnie. For the fact is—and this is something that nobody, oddly enough, has ever picked up on—Ronnie has always been a very competitive person. He has never needed to be "pushed."

A Presidential Love Letter on Their Anniversary[*]

THE WHITE HOUSE
WASHINGTON   March 4, 1981

Dear First Lady
As Pres. Of the U.S., it is my honor & privilege to cite you for service above & beyond the call of duty in that you have made one man (me) the most happy man in the world for 29 years.

Beginning in 1951, Nancy Davis, seeing the plight of a lonely man who didn't know how lonely he really was, determined to rescue him from a completely empty life. Refusing to be rebuffed by a certain amount of stupidity on his part she ignored his somewhat slow response. With patience & tenderness she gradually brought the light of understanding to his darkened, obtuse mind and he discovered the joy of loving someone with all his heart.

Nancy Davis then went on to bring him happiness for the next 29 years as Nancy Davis Reagan for which she has received & will continue to receive his undying devotion forever & ever.

She has done this in spite of the fact that he still can't find the words to tell her how lost he would be without her. He sits in the Oval office from which he can see (if he scrooches down) her window and feels warm all over just knowing she is there.

The above is the statement of the man who benefited from her act of heroism.

The below is his signature.

Ronald Reagan

Ronald Reagan—Pres. of the U.S.
P.S. He—I mean I, love and adore you.

*The original letter was handwritten, as were most of the letters Reagan wrote to Nancy.

PRIVATE TIME AS GOVERNOR

I KNEW IT WAS VERY IMPORTANT FOR RONNIE, at the end of each day, to be able to put politics behind him and come home to his peaceful life with the children and me. He didn't like to go out after work, to stop off at Frank Fat's—the place everyone else in government went to for a drink. It had been that same way when he was in pictures—he never stayed around and had a drink with the fellows in the dressing room. He just came home. And in Sacramento, he wanted to close the door of his office and walk away. I think this helped keep him sane in the turbulent years of the sixties and early seventies, when the world seemed to go crazy.

WHAT PASSES FOR PRESIDENTIAL SOLITUDE

WHILE WE WERE IN THE WHITE HOUSE we spent as much time as we could together. Whenever we could, we made weekend trips to Camp David. Camp David! When I think about it now, it seems like another life—which, I guess, it was. It was such a wonderful place…. When we first started going out there, it needed some work. I did some gardening and some work on the cabins, which I really enjoyed. And Ronnie enjoyed himself in his own usual ways—being outside and riding, in particular. The Secret Service didn't want him going too far at first, but as time went by, he'd suggest adding a little more to the trail and then a bit more and a bit more, until, by the end, he had the kind of substantial ride he was used to.

Sometimes, just the two of us went to Camp David (that is to say, the two of us plus the Secret Service, the White House doctor, someone from the press office, and other White House staff—that's solitude during the presidency). Sometimes Ron and his new wife, Doria, would come, or a couple of close friends, like Charles and Mary Jane Wick and their children. But we never made a big social event out of it. What we really enjoyed doing there was relaxing,

wearing blue jeans, reading, riding horses, watching movies—just generally doing the kinds of things that we'd always done on the ranch back home.

I think that's largely why we didn't find Washington strange or lonely the way many people who move there from other places say they do. We were still together all the time, and we were still us—with Ronnie on the left side of the bed and me on the right, waking up with our breakfast trays and our King Charles spaniel, Rex, a gift from Pat and Bill Buckley, jumping into bed between us. We added many new people to our lives who are still friends. Of course, living in the White House, if we wanted to make new friends, we had to reach out—just as anyone who moved to a new city has to do.

Making these new friends and bringing them home to Ronnie was part of the fun for me, and a big part of what I saw my job to be as first lady.

Letters
Reagan writes to family and friends

'LOVE IS NOT A MAGIC TOUCH OF COSMIC DUST'
Dec. 17, 1951, to a friend who had recently divorced her husband

YOUR LETTER LED ME TO BELIEVE YOU are embarked on a course which can only lead to unhappiness and a barren future and this is all wrong. You are young and very attractive and have a great deal to offer some worthwhile man and both you and your son need a man in your life or lives....

You say you believe there is one love in life for each of us—this is just not true. Can you believe that God means for millions of really young people to go on through life alone because a war robbed them of their first loves? Maybe you'll resent this Florence but I must say it—you have to look into your own heart and ask yourself if you really believe in one love now lost to you or if this is a shield behind which you hide because your past experience did not measure up to your girlhood dreams and now you fear men....

The world is full of lonely people—people capable of happiness and of giving happiness and love is not a magic touch of cosmic dust that preordains two people and two people only for each other. Love can grow slowly out of warmth and companionship and none of us should be afraid to seek it.

'TAKE CARE OF MOMMIE'
July 12, 1954, from a Montana movie set to daughter Patti

PRETTY SOON THE MOON AND THE STARS and this breeze got together and filled me with a longing so great that it seemed I'd die of pain if I couldn't reach out and touch your Mommie. You aren't old enough to really understand what I mean but you will someday. Right now just imagine what you feel like when you want "num num" real bad and it isn't in sight and when you want to hold Teddy real tight—put this all together, double it and it is just a faint hint of how I feel.

Maybe it's a good thing to be apart now and then. Not that I have to be away from our Mommie to know how much I love her but a thirst now and then makes you know and remember how really sweet the water is.

I'm counting on you to take care of Mommie and keep her safe for me because there wouldn't be any moon or stars in the sky without her.

'RETURN TO SANITY AND LAW AND ORDER'

June 5, 1968, to Patti after Robert F. Kennedy was shot

I'VE BEEN HERE IN THE OFFICE ALL DAY, and feeling almost sick most of the time. Even though I disagree with him on political matters and even though I disapprove of him and his approach to these problems, I still feel very deeply the tragedy of this young man taken from his family in this way. I don't mean to make this sound so final, but the latest word we've been getting is one that the condition is very grave....

In all of this sometimes one can learn why a certain course has been followed. There are many times when I have wondered why I'm doing what I'm doing. Now is one of those moments when I'm grateful that I can be in a position to perhaps change things to see that we do start a return to sanity and law and order and turn away from this whole creed of violence that seems to be so prevalent in our land.

'NO GREATER HAPPINESS'

June 1971, advising son Michael how to stay happily married

THERE IS AN OLD LAW OF PHYSICS that you can only get out of a thing as much as you put in it. The man who puts into the marriage only half of what he owns will get that out. Sure, there will be moments when you will see someone or think back on an earlier time and you will be challenged to see if you can still make the grade, but let me tell you how really great is the challenge of proving your masculinity and charm with one woman for the rest of your life. Any man can find a twerp here and there who will go along with cheating, and it doesn't take all that much manhood. It does take quite a man to remain attractive and to be loved by a woman who has heard him snore, seen him unshaven, tended him while he was sick and washed his dirty underwear. Do that and keep her still feeling a warm glow and you will know some very beautiful music....

Mike, you know better than many what an unhappy home is and what it can do to others. Now you have a chance to make it come out the way it should. There is no greater happiness for a man than approaching a door at the end of a day knowing someone on the other side of that door is waiting for the sounds of his footsteps.

BUILDING YOUR 'CHARACTER MUSCLE'

Circa 1972, to son Ron after a bad report card

THIS PERIOD OF THE SCHOOL YEAR, whether it be high school or college, is the toughest. Don't ask me why, but it's always been true. This is when the excitement of fall and starting the new year seems a long way back and the summer an even longer way ahead. It's easy to get bored, to complain about everything and to think the school and everyone connected with it are out to ruin your life. This is when you have to remember the price for giving up and copping out. It's also the time when you build some character muscle to see you through real problems that come along later in life. And they do come along.

It's only a few years now (they seem many to you) until you'll be out of school and really beginning your life. All that has gone before and these remaining few years of school and college are "spring training" for the real season. When we are young we look at adults going about their day-to-day work and it all seems pretty dull and uninteresting. Believe me, that isn't so. I can't remember a time since graduation when I've been bored. Finding the thing you want to do and making a go of it is next in importance to finding the person you want to share your life with.

'I ENJOYED EVERY SCRATCH'

Sept. 15, 1981, to a Wyoming couple after a stay on his California ranch

WE HAD A FREAK STORM IN THE SPRING that dumped eight inches of wet snow on the ranch, and I think there must be ten thousand oak limbs and trees that were downed by that heavy snow. Although we couldn't use all that firewood in the next 20 years, most of our afternoons were spent with chainsaws, jeep, and trailer, cutting off the little limbs and saving the logs for firewood. We brushpiled the other and are waiting for the rainy season to burn it....

Nevertheless, it was fun, and I enjoyed every scratch and bruise and sore muscle.

The Hollywood Years

PICTURES PREPARED HIM FOR POLITICS

BY ROBERT F. HOWE

Robert F. Howe is a former writer and editor at the Baltimore Sun, *the* Washington Post *and* People *magazine.*

PURRING INTO TOWN IN HIS NASH CONVERTIBLE, Ronald Reagan arrived in "Tinseltown" in 1937 as a wide-eyed, cheerful, moralistic, optimistic 26-year-old. That is the way the movie community saw him, and, for that matter, it was pretty much how he saw himself. He was determined, too—determined to make it in the movies.

He quickly landed his first part in the caper comedy *Love Is on the Air* and wrapped up his career 27 years later with *The Killers* in an ill-fitting role as a mob boss. Judged solely on talent, Reagan's career would have to be described as competent more than distinguished. "Competent," however, by no means suggests "unsuccessful." He appeared in more than 60 films, succeeding far beyond his dreams.

More important, Hollywood transformed him. He maintained much of his moral optimism in later years, but he was no longer the guileless youth from the heartland. He had become a popular movie star who moved among the rich and famous and liked it, becoming wealthy himself and troubled for the first time by such side effects of success as high taxes. He would also serve seven terms as president of the Screen Actors Guild, fighting for much-needed actors' benefits and on occasion supporting strikes, even as he denied the existence of an anti-communist Hollywood blacklist and edged further to the political right.

He also spent the equivalent of two of his eight years as host of the popular television show *General Electric Theater* touring the nation as a company man to talk shop, and politics, with General Electric employees and customers. Through all these experiences, he learned how to cultivate a following, sharpened his conservative ideology and his skills of political negotiation, and evolved into a comfortably eloquent, and often witty and self-deprecating, speaker.

Future political foes would try to leverage the fact that Reagan had been an actor to trivialize him with voters. Instead, Hollywood helped prepare him for the political stage, serving almost as a glorified screen test in a run for the loftiest role of all.

THE BUDDING STAR

IT WAS NO EASY TASK FOR THE SMALL-TOWN Midwestern native to get traction in Hollywood. He had distinguished himself in radio, gaining experience and presence in a medium that was burgeoning at about the same time as talking pictures. He also gained confidence when he was sent to big cities as a touring sportscaster. But he had spent little meaningful time on the stage. Still, Warner Bros. seemed not to mind, gave him a screen test and signed him to a contract.

This was the era when studios pretty much owned the actors, dictating especially to newcomers what roles to play and when. Earning the equivalent of an actor's minimum wage, he made 13 movies in his first 18 months. One was *Hollywood Hotel*, in which he had an unbilled bit part as a radio announcer. The movie was a spoof of the film business, with the action centered on a fictional studio called Miracle Pictures. Its slogan was "If it's a good picture, it's a miracle." In a way, that's how Reagan's first two years in Hollywood could be summed up. He either had small parts in big pictures or big parts in small pictures, none of them memorable.

But two early films would prove to be important to the young actor. The first was *The Amazing Dr. Clitterhouse*, in 1938, a sendup of the gangster genre with Edward G. Robinson, Humphrey Bogart and Claire Trevor. John Huston co-wrote the screenplay. Reagan was billed only as "announcer's voice," but the film introduced him to the famous Huston family of Hollywood. Their paths would cross again.

That same year, Reagan landed a substantial role as a VMI student in a buddy picture called *Brother Rat*. In a co-star he also found a girlfriend, pretty Jane Wyman, an ambitious young actress who intended to work her way out of a typecasting rut of pert and perky roles.

She would find help on that front from the supremely influential gossip columnist Louella Parsons, who also happened to hail from Reagan's hometown of Dixon, Ill. She liked Reagan and Wyman and took them on a "Stars of Tomorrow" vaudeville tour in 1939. Not long after, Parsons announced their engagement in her column, then paid for their wedding reception on Jan. 26, 1940.

By then, Reagan was getting some notice. He received fourth billing in a major film, *Dark Victory*, in 1939, with Bette Davis and Humphrey Bogart. Reviews paid him little mind, describing his efforts as "dependable," but the experience gave his career a boost. He also campaigned hard that year for a spot in 1940's *Knute Rockne—All American*. Reagan loved the story of Notre Dame's famous football coach and coveted the role of his ill-starred standout player, George Gipp. He landed the part and delivered one of the two immortal lines he would contribute to Hollywood lore—and to his own legacy: "Win one for the Gipper."

After *Knute Rockne*, Reagan's roles were upgraded, and he even managed to steal a few scenes from Errol Flynn in the 1942 drama *Desperate Journey*—no small feat. He had irked Flynn in 1940's *Santa Fe Trail* as well. Recalled co-star Olivia de Havilland, "Errol was nettled by Ronnie's popularity on the set."

WARTIME IN HOLLYWOOD

WITH THE ARRIVAL OF THE 1940S came vast changes for the nation and for Reagan. The world had yet to fully recover from the Great Depression, and war had broken out in Europe and the Far East. U.S. involvement would not be long in coming. Now that he was an established professional as well as a father, Reagan's worldview expanded. In politics, he was still a loyal Democrat and an active union man who would soon be swept into military service. In the midst of all this, he was about to give the best performance of his career. The picture was *Kings Row*, in 1942, in which he played Drake McHugh, a trust-fund dandy who loses his money, then his legs.

Everything about this film was first rate. Sam Wood directed, and the script brought out the best in Robert Cummings, Ann Sheridan, Claude Rains, Judith Anderson and others. There were three Academy Award nominations for *Kings Row*: best picture, best director and best cinematographer. But *Mrs. Miniver*, an early portrait of the war directed by William Wyler, took all three. Hollywood's attention was consumed by World War II.

There was a write-in campaign for Reagan as best supporting actor, but nothing came of it. Still, he delivered his second immortal film line. When his character awakens after a train accident to find his legs have been amputated, he cries out in anguish, "Where's the rest of me?" That became the title of his 1965 autobiography. Reagan himself was quoted as saying, "Perhaps I never did quite as well again in a single shot."

Restricted from combat service because of bad eyesight, Reagan, an Army reservist since 1937, entered active duty in 1942. He helped make 400 training films and one patriotic movie, *This Is the Army*, in 1943, and was soon promoted to captain. He and Wyman were now often touted on magazine covers as the perfect couple—a young serviceman and his working wife.

Wyman's campaign for better parts was paying off as the war wound down. She earned a solid supporting role in 1945's Academy Award–winning *The Lost Weekend*, a serious look at alcoholism. It was a familiar subject to many of the Reagans' colleagues. They once spent a Christmas holiday with John Huston and his wife, Evelyn Keyes, and, according to Keyes, John and Jane got "sloshed" on beer and Reagan was displeased: "Ronnie was very straitlaced. He took over the driving. I sat beside him and the two gigglers were in the back. He said, 'Evelyn, let's be the policemen.'"

The postwar era proved a challenge to many actors. Movie-goers' tastes had changed, and Reagan got off to a shaky start with a couple of clunkers, including 1947's *Stallion Road* in which he played a besotted veterinarian. He rebounded later that year with *The Voice of the Turtle*, a comedy in which Reagan, a soldier on leave, is thrown together with a pretty young woman—a commercial success that earned his best reviews since *Kings Row*. In the world of unintended consequences, this film also caused him to miss out on working on a film he really wanted: *The Treasure of the Sierra Madre*, with actor Walter Huston and director John Huston. John made the offer, but Warner Bros. forbade Reagan to accept it.

Another meaty role came his way in 1949's *Hasty Heart*, shot in a still-ravaged postwar England. Unfortunately, Reagan, playing a wounded soldier, and director Vincent Sherman were at odds over a scene in which the director believed Reagan had not shown enough emotional depth. He demanded more and more takes, long after Reagan believed he had struck the right tone. In the end, actor Richard Todd received an Academy Award nomination and Reagan was again overlooked.

Reagan did not forget. In his book, *Where's the Rest of Me?*, he gave glowing reports of the actors, the writers and the technicians on the film but mentioned not one word about his director.

As Reagan's career faltered, his wife's soared. Following *The Lost Weekend*, Wyman landed a plum role in the much-anticipated 1946 film *The Yearling*. Cast as a distraught mother who had lost three children, she was nominated for best actress. She lost to Olivia de Havilland in *To Each His Own*, but went on to win for her role as a mute in 1948's *Johnny Belinda*. Wyman was now in an entirely different category from her husband, and the fissures in their marriage were soon brutally exposed for all to see. She filed for divorce in June 1948.

He was devastated but, when asked to comment on the divorce, found the will to make light of it, responding, "I think I'll name *Johnny Belinda* as co-respondent."

NANCY ENTERS THE PICTURE

OVER THE NEXT 16 YEARS, Reagan would appear in 21 more films. One of his personal favorites was *The Winning Team* in 1952, a biopic on the life of baseball great Grover Cleveland Alexander. The film might be best remembered for a remark Reagan made shortly after being elected president. Making a courtesy call to Democratic Speaker of the House Tip O'Neill, Reagan admired the speaker's fine oak desk. Pleased, O'Neill informed him that it had once belonged to Grover Cleveland (famous for being the only president ever to serve two nonconsecutive terms). Reagan lit up and said, "You know, I once played Grover Cleveland in the movies." "No, Mr. President," O'Neill said, "you're thinking of Grover Cleveland Alexander, the ballplayer."

More important than any of his movies, during this or any period, a powerful new force had entered Reagan's life, one that would far outlast his acting career: Nancy Davis.

Their first encounter was anything but glamorous. Davis called Reagan in 1949 because he was the president of the Screen Actors Guild and she needed help in a matter of mistaken identity. In the heated anti-communist fervor of the late 1940s, Davis had been mistaken for a woman with the same name who had been accused of subversive activity, and Davis, an actress, was having trouble getting jobs. Reagan went to work clearing up the misunderstanding. He also went to work getting to know Davis better.

Coincidentally, Nancy enjoyed a longtime association with a family who had become a part of Reagan's life—the Hustons. John Huston even gave a dinner party at Chasen's restaurant to welcome her to Hollywood. When she had been a child, her father, Dr. Loyal Davis, became a close friend of the Huston patriarch, Walter, one of the best actors of the 20th century.

Nancy called him "Uncle Walter." When he performed in the hit Broadway musical *Knickerbocker Holiday* and sang the immortal "September Song" for a group of Los Angeles friends, he called Nancy his "best audience." She and the Hustons would remain close for many years, even as Reagan veered further right politically and the Hustons clung firmly to the left. During Reagan's second term as president, Nancy tried to get John Huston to concede that her husband had been a better president than he thought possible. "No, Nancy," he replied. "Worse. Much worse."

From 1948 to 1958 Nancy made 11 films, and in the middle, in 1952, she married Reagan. They co-starred in just one motion picture, *Hellcats of the Navy*, in 1957, and she rounded out her career in 1958 with *Crash Landing*. But by then, she was well into the life's work that would define her: helping her husband succeed.

In retrospect, Reagan wished that *Hellcats* had been his last film. Instead it was *The Killers*, released in 1964. For the first time he played a genuine villain. This iteration of Ernest Hemingway's short story is deeply violent and cynical. Reagan is killed in the story, and it is far from a heroic death. He is said to have regretted playing the part. Some even thought it might damage his nascent political career. They need not have worried. Few people saw it.

In the end, Reagan was never a great actor. But for his larger purpose in 20th-century America, he was something more important. He was a movie star—one who had soaked up dialogue and, with his prodigious memory, filed the words away for a time when they might be needed.

A LOYAL UNION MAN

AFTER WORLD WAR I AND THROUGH THE 1920S, a typical American's goal was to get rich, the quicker the better. Successful businessmen were heroes, and Calvin Coolidge spoke for much of the country when he said, "The business of America is business."

Then business failed the nation, spectacularly.

In a wink of time, the American hero became "the common man." Egalitarianism was in and conspicuous consumption out, except as a horrible example, as in *My Man Godfrey*. Hit movies had titles like *Mr. Deeds Goes to Town, Meet John Doe, Stand Up and Cheer, Mr. Smith Goes to Washington* and *The Grapes of Wrath*. Banks could be redeemed only if they were hometown savings and loans, as in *It's a Wonderful Life*, where the banker lived pretty much the way his depositors did.

This turn of events fit Reagan well. His politics then were as much populist as party-bound, and he described himself as "Mr. Norm"—a man who tended to see the best in people and expected the best for the country.

Unions and new labor laws were in the news, and organized labor also suited Reagan. He had shown a political streak as a youth, came from a pro-union family and even joined in a student strike in college. He signed up with SAG in 1937 and was quick at meetings to stand and give a speech, often a good speech.

He moved up in the ranks quickly, with Wyman's help and encouragement—ironic, since she would later cite his preoccupation with SAG in her divorce proceedings. He became a member of the board of directors as an alternate in 1941 and was elected third vice president in 1946.

In March 1947 several board members, including president Robert Montgomery, resigned as a result of tougher SAG bylaws forbidding guild officials to hold management or investment roles in films; they drafted Reagan to fulfill Montgomery's term. Then, between 1947 and 1959, the full SAG membership elected him to six one-year terms.

For the most part, Reagan neatly straddled the line between the actors and the producers who held their contracts. But that balance was tested as the House Un-American Activities Committee grew increasingly suspicious of the movie business, alleging that communists had infiltrated at troublesome levels. Ten writers and directors who were called to testify before the committee refused to cooperate and, on Nov. 24, 1947, were found in contempt. The next day Hollywood executives fired them, and the Hollywood blacklist was born.

There was never a literal list, but it was clear that people were being denied work because of their political affiliations—or alleged affiliations. Reagan, though increasingly anti-communist, trod a middle ground. On one hand, he denied the existence of a blacklist, arguing essentially that it was an unfortunate byproduct of public taste. If the public refused to see films made by actors and directors they thought were traitors, went his rationale, why should producers have to hire those people, fully expecting audiences to steer clear and the movies to fail?

On the other hand, he was hardly in thrall to the committee, which he called "a pretty venal bunch." When he appeared before the committee the month before the contempt findings, he conceded that there was a "small clique" within SAG who followed "the tactics we associate with the Communist Party." Pressed to explain how communist sympathizers could be prevented from holding undue influence in SAG, he said the best approach was to let democracy do its work; they would be voted out. Sticking up for the ultimate principle of freedom of choice, he later boldly added, "As a citizen I would hesitate, or not like, to see any political party outlawed on the basis of its political ideology."

As a side note, it is intriguing to know that Reagan and Wyman had secretly agreed in April of that year to serve as informants for the FBI, reporting communist activity in the ranks of Hollywood. Reagan, code-named T-10, did express his reservations, saying, "Do they expect us to constitute ourselves as a little FBI of our own and determine just who is a commie and who isn't?" There is no evidence that he reported anyone who was not already known to the bureau.

CALL TO THE FUTURE: TELEVISION

BY THE MID-1950S, REAGAN WOULD NEED to reinvent himself in earnest. His film career was all but over, his commitment to SAG was winding down and, in 1952, Nancy gave birth to their first child, Patti. The solution: television.

Like other prominent actors of his generation, Reagan had seen television as a threat—and with good reason. Theater audiences shrank as fans stayed home to watch their heroes for free on the tube. As need or opportunity arose, Reagan began to dabble, appearing now and then on the *Schlitz Playhouse, Ford Television Theatre, The George Burns and Gracie Allen Show* and other programs.

Then came *General Electric Theater*, and Reagan was all in. He agreed to be the host, appearing only occasionally in an episode. In 1958, for instance, he and Nancy co-starred in a story called "A Turkey for the President."

It was a sweetheart deal, made possible with a little help from his friends. In 1952, when he was still president of SAG, Reagan signed an agreement with the Music Corporation of America (MCA) that allowed the company to produce television shows. It was a startling exemption from SAG bylaws that had kept actors and agents who produced movies at arm's length; MCA had been primarily a talent agency and now wanted to go into production in earnest. To sweeten the pot, it promised SAG it would secure additional fees (residuals) for television actors when their shows were repeated—something actors had wanted for years.

Reagan argued that the waiver provided widening opportunities in television: "I was for anyone that could give employment." No doubt true, but questions were raised because he had brokered the MCA deal while MCA represented him. Two years later, Reagan, though no longer president, voted in favor of a permanent extension of the agreement. That same year he was named host of *GE Theater*, one of MCA's most successful programs. MCA even negotiated with GE over his contract—$125,000 a year. A heady bit of money in those days.

Residuals came up again in 1960, with SAG arguing that motion-picture actors should also receive compensation when their films were aired on television. Producers resisted, and Reagan called for a strike. After a brief walkout, a settlement was reached that promised residuals for movies made starting in 1960. The deal also provided a one-time payout for films made between 1948 and 1959 to be used to fund a health and pension plan. Older stars like Bob Hope and Glenn Ford were furious with the paltry sum, but the majority welcomed the pension and health coverage. The later SAG president Melissa Gilbert spoke for most actors when she praised Reagan's work representing their interests—despite her observation that his "politics grew conservative over the years and, at times, at odds with the nation's labor movement."

GE wanted more than a host for Reagan's comfortable salary, so despite his fear of airplanes he became a glorified pitchman for the company, traveling by train all over the country to visit dealers and speak to their plant workers. At first he entertained them with an endless supply of Hollywood anecdotes. But that wouldn't last. The transformation of Ronald Reagan was not complete.

Leaving the confines of Hollywood, he found himself shaking hands with the type of people he grew up with. His life was quite different from theirs now, but his audience felt a connection. And they were interested in more than movies. They wanted to know what he thought of big business and government, and he was happy to oblige. His talks grew more political—and conservative. The onetime New Deal booster now delivered speeches laced with barbs suggesting that government was part of the problem, not the solution.

Reagan was in high demand, and GE, its brand reaping the rewards, gave him liberty to say pretty much what he pleased. In 1960 the Republicans came calling, asking that he endorse Richard Nixon—and requesting that he remain with the Democratic Party so the PR impact might be greater. Reagan had vigorously opposed Nixon in 1950 when Democrat Helen Gahagan Douglas ran unsuccessfully against him for a Senate seat. But now Reagan was in Nixon's corner and did as he was asked, waiting until 1962 to register Republican.

The reasons given for Reagan's departure from *GE Theater* in 1962 vary. Ratings may have played a role, and he had reportedly bridled when a GE boss asked him to drop the policy talks and stick to praising company products. Regardless of the reason, Reagan came out the winner. He was considerably better off financially, he had honed his conservative ideals in his countless talks and, in terms of exposure, he had pressed more flesh than any but the most prominent political candidates.

For years, film critics had used similar adjectives to describe Reagan. Affable. Genial. Handsome. Reliable. Square. Professional. Stolid. Disarming. Supportive. Actors might not consider all these descriptions entirely positive. On the other hand, those attributes could serve a politician well. All he had to do was convince people that an actor could also be a leader.

One public official who saw that very potential early on was liberal Republican senator John Sherman Cooper of Kentucky. When Reagan won the hearts of Californians as governor, Sherman gave the former actor one of his strongest reviews: "He's dangerous, because he's a nice guy. People like him. He's comfortable on a big stage. He could go all the way."

Special thanks to Nick Clooney, former host of American Movie Classics, *for sharing his insights into Hollywood.*

What the Critics Said

Real-time reviews were positive, but decidedly subdued

BROTHER RAT (1938)

THREE FIRST CLASSMEN, Wayne Morris, Eddie Albert and Ronald Regan [*sic*], involve themselves in a series of escapades that keep them moving fast until final diplomas are received. Things start when the girls arrive for the big baseball game, prom and commencement. Morris and Regan [*sic*] skip quarters to romance Priscilla Lane and Jane Wyman, while Albert goes into a trance when he finds he is to become a father....

Wayne Morris provides a good characterization of the unreliable and take-a-chance cadet whose decisions continually keep the trio in hot water. Ronald Regan [*sic*] is fine as the third member of the group, while Priscilla Lane, Jane Wyman and Jane Bryan are nicely cast for the romantic interest.

—*Variety*, Oct. 19, 1938

DARK VICTORY (1939)

THE GOOD POINTS SO FAR OUTNUMBER the weaknesses of *Dark Victory*.... Heading them is Miss [Bette] Davis' characterization of a young woman who learns she has but a few months to live.... Miss Davis fashions from that bit of dramatic circumstance an intensity which makes *Dark Victory* exceptionally gripping at nearly all times.... There are also Humphrey Bogart and such dependables as Cora Witherspoon, Ronald Reagan and others to make up what the script calls the "station wagon crowd."

—*Wall Street Journal*, April 21, 1939

KNUTE ROCKNE—ALL AMERICAN (1940)

FOR DYED-IN-THE-WOOL FOOTBALL FANS and alumni of Notre Dame, whether they be of the genuine or just plain "subway"

Sparks flew between Reagan and his Brother Rat *co-star Jane Wyman (top).
Diva Bette Davis (above, to his right, in* Dark Victory) *called Reagan "Little Ronnie."*

variety, this glowing, heroic account of the great coach's life and noble works will be much more than entertainment. It will be an effective inspiration....

If some of it is largely sentimental and on the mock-heroic side—such as the scene in which the famous George Gipp [Reagan], on his death-bed, whispers to Rockne, "Some day, when things are tough, maybe you can ask the boys to go in there and win just once for the Gipper"; if some of it is slightly juvenile, that's all a part of the sport. And that also makes it one of the best pictures for boys in years.

—*New York Times*, Oct. 19, 1940

KINGS ROW (1942)

KINGS ROW, HENRY BELLAMANN'S WIDELY-READ novel of small-town life at the turn of the century, becomes an impressive and occasionally inspiring, though overlong picture under Sam Wood's eloquent direction....

It also covers the frustrated romance of the hero's friend [Reagan], the latter's loss of his fortune and the subsequent amputation of both legs after an accident....

Ronald Reagan does a continuously believeable job in the like-able, relatively simple part of the hero's colorful, courageous friend.

—*Variety*, Dec. 24, 1941

BEDTIME FOR BONZO (1951)

THE AUTHORS AND SCENARISTS have peppered the goings-on with a few professional phrases, such as "inverted psycho-domination," but all it amounts to is the attempt by a youthful psychology professor [Reagan] to show that "a lot of people think they're born better than others, but I think it's the way they're raised." And to prove his case he enlists Bonzo as a sort of primate "guinea pig." ...

Ronald Reagan, as the professor; Diana Lynn, as Bonzo's "momma"; Walter Slezak, as Reagan's sympathetic colleague,

Five months before Knute Rockne—All American *debuted, Warner Bros. unveiled "the Gipper" for L.A. art students to admire (top). Reagan's* Kings Row *performance (above) earned him a million-dollar Warner Bros. contract.*

and Lucille Barkley, as the Dean's cool and intellectual daughter, work hard but obviously ineffectively. They haven't a chance since Bonzo makes monkeys of them all.

—*New York Times*, April 6, 1951

CATTLE QUEEN OF MONTANA (1954)

ACCOUTERED IN SPLIT SKIRTS and off-the-face Stetson, [Barbara Stanwyck] is as photogenic as any lady pioneer has a right to be. But it is her misfortune to discover that there are dastardly cattlemen among the decent settlers in the old Montana territory, and that there are villainous, whiskey-slugging Blackfoot braves among the upstanding warriors who want to be at peace with the white man....

Meanwhile, of course, Ronald Reagan is working with the Army to uncover the schemers who are playing hob with the peaceable Blackfoot.

It should not take an explosion like that climactically engineered by Mr. Reagan to expose the rickety bones of the rest of this standard plot.... Mr. Reagan is stalwart and obvious as her protector.

—*New York Times*, Jan. 26, 1955

HELLCATS OF THE NAVY (1957)

THE 1944 SUBMARINE OPERATION in the Tsushima Strait and Sea of Japan backgrounds *Hellcats of the Navy*. The underwater fighting is laced with formula plot which at times gets awfully trite, but results are still okay for the general dual-bill situation....

Ronald Reagan is the sub commander around whom the Navy underseas operation pivots. He plays it sternly, without being the typical film version of a martinet.... Nancy Davis is the nurse waiting on shore for Reagan to make up his mind about marriage—a thankless role.

—*Variety*, May 1, 1957

The chimp stole the show in Bedtime for Bonzo *(top left). Reagan and Nancy appeared together on the silver screen just once, in* Hellcats of the Navy *(top right). On set in Montana, Barbara Stanwyck and Reagan face off in* Cattle Queen *(above).*

A mobster and his moll (Reagan and Angie Dickinson) meet bloody ends in *The Killers,* Reagan's last picture.

THE KILLERS (1964)

ONLY THE MOST DEVOTED BUFFS of the crime melodrama will get much of a charge out of this exercise in hate, double-cross and sadism....

Of the actors, [John] Cassavetes and Clu Gulager come off best, the former arousing interest with his customary histrionic drive and intensity, the latter fashioning a colorful study in evil, a portrait of playful sadism.... Ronald Reagan fails to crash convincingly through his good-guy image in his portrayal of a ruthless crook.

—*Variety,* June 3, 1964

Letters

Reagan writes about the world of Hollywood

'I PUT NO STOCK IN THESE RUMORS'

May 3, 1950, to studio boss Jack L. Warner

I KNOW THAT YOU WILL RECALL our discussion some time ago with regard to *That Hagen Girl*. You agreed the script and role were very weak but asked me to do the picture as a personal favor which I gladly did. At that time you encouraged me to bring in a suitable outdoor script which you agreed to buy as a starring vehicle for me. I found such a property in *Ghost Mountain* and the studio purchased it with me....

Of late there have been "gossip items" indicating you intend to star someone else in this story. Naturally I put no stock in these rumors—I know you too well to ever think you'd break your word.

However I am anxious to know something of production plans—starting date, etc. in order to better schedule my own plans. Frankly I hope it is soon.

[*Editor's note: The title was changed to* Rocky Mountain, *and the film starred Errol Flynn.*]

'HOLLYWOOD HAS NO BLACKLIST'

July 4, 1960, to Hugh Hefner in response to a Playboy *piece criticizing the Hollywood "blacklist"*

I, LIKE YOU, WILL DEFEND THE RIGHT of any American to openly practice and preach any political philosophy from monarchy to anarchy. But this is not the case with regard to the communist. He is bound by party discipline to deny he is a communist so that he can by subversion and stealth impose on an unwilling people the rule of the International Communist Party which is in fact the government of Soviet Russia. I say to you that any man still or now a member of the "party" was a man who looked upon the death of American soldiers in Korea as a victory for his side....

Hollywood has no blacklist. Hollywood does have a list handed to it by millions of "moviegoers" who have said "we don't want and will not pay to see pictures made by or with these people we consider traitors." On this list were many names of people we in Hollywood felt were wrongly suspect. I personally served on a committee that succeeded in clearing these people....

I must ask you as a publisher, aside from any questions of political philosophy, should a film producer be accused of bigotry for not hiring an artist when the customers for his product have labeled the artist "poor box office," regardless of the cause?

'I'LL REQUIRE PSYCHIATRIC CARE'

Sept. 4, 1968, to Bob Hope, asking him to attend a governors' conference
I'VE WANTED FOR A LONG TIME a legitimate occasion for paying tribute to you on behalf of our state. I know this sounds a h--l of a lot like, "be my guest but bring your music," but even with an "honorary degree" you have to make a speech so I'll pretend I'm not self-conscious....

Now beyond all this let me just add that if it is impossible for you we'll still love you. Oh Nancy will probably be inconsolable for two or three years, I'll require psychiatric care and our children will probably be taken from us to be put in a foster home. [Democrat] Jesse Unruh might even become governor.

PATTON 'SAYS THINGS THAT NEED SAYING'

March 10, 1970, to film producer and retired general Frank McCarthy
NANCY AND THE SKIPPER [SON RON] AND I saw *Patton* Saturday night. I told you once I would hate anyone who ever played that role other than myself. Now I hate George Scott for proving that no one in the world but him could ever have played the part.

Frank, it is a magnificent piece of picture making and it says some things that very much need saying today. I have been greatly disturbed for some time over the pernicious and constant degrading of the military. This picture restored a great deal of balance. I don't know whether Patton would ever be the kind of man you'd want to take on a picnic, but I do thank God that when trouble came, there were men like him around. I'm really too full of the picture yet to make specific comments other than to say it has been many years since I have so completely lost myself in a picture.

'MOUNT OLYMPUS FOR THE THEATRICAL GREAT'

July 29, 1970, to director George Marshall

I'LL ALWAYS BE GRATEFUL that I knew Hollywood in the "Golden Era" when it was big and brash and confident it could do anything—and usually did. It also was the Hollywood that became Mount Olympus for the world's theatrical great.

In that time the greatest pool of theatrical skill and talent that has ever been assembled anywhere was the community datelined "Hollywood." At the same time it was a place of friendship and warmth.

'NO PLACE' FOR GOVERNMENT CENSORSHIP

Circa 1970s, to a friend who asked for his view on censorship

TRUTH IS I HAVE SOME RATHER STRONG FEELINGS about much of what is being offered on the screen and tube of late. Yes there have been some good and inspirational stories but even these are too often tarnished by dialogue laced with profanity and vulgarities to say nothing of the inevitable bedroom scene which leaves little to the imagination....

What to do about it? Well one thing that must not be done is to open the door to government censorship. Anyone with the character to be a good censor would have too much character to be one. There is no place in our free society for government at any level to impose itself on the theater....

Let the industry itself adopt, as it did many years ago, a voluntary code of ethics and behavior based on good taste and simple morality. Who knows—we might see another "Golden Era" when pictures would once again be the major entertainment for the entire family.

THE GIPPER 'REMAINED A PART OF MY LIFE'

May 22, 1986, to a fan asking about "the Gipper"

YOU WONDERED ABOUT GIPP and whether this might be a forgotten part of my past. Quite the contrary. He has remained very much a part of my life, indeed playing him was the role that moved me into the star category. Curious enough, at political rallies during my last campaign there would always be signs out in the crowd referring to me as "The Gipper." And believe me, I liked that very much.

The Governor

THE CALIFORNIA PROVING GROUND

BY LOU CANNON

ON NOV. 18, 1980, TWO WEEKS AFTER HE WAS elected president of the United States, Ronald Reagan traveled to Washington, D.C., to meet with Thomas P. (Tip) O'Neill, the Democratic speaker of the House of Representatives. Baiting the president-elect, O'Neill told him his legislative proposals might be slower to move in Washington than they had been in California, where Reagan had served as governor for eight years. O'Neill, a baseball fan, called California "the minor leagues" of politics. "This is the big leagues," he said.

O'Neill underestimated Reagan, as the speaker acknowledged the next year, after the president maneuvered his ambitious economic program through the Democratic-controlled House. He also underrated California, then a turbulent microcosm of the United States.

In the 1960s the Golden State was a hotbed of rebellion—on campus at U.C. Berkeley, in the crowded ghettos of Oakland and Watts, and on the industrialized farms of the Central Valley where farmworkers were struggling to organize. State government was on the cutting edge of change. During Reagan's governorship Sacramento was a laboratory for controversial policy decisions on abortion, air pollution, tax relief and welfare reform.

Mirroring Washington, Sacramento had a potent corps of lobbyists and a robust permanent government staffed by career bureaucrats protected by civil service. Sacramento also resembled Washington in another way that would be crucial to the political education of Governor Reagan: Democrats controlled the Legislature, where the most powerful figure was Assembly Speaker Jesse (Big Daddy) Unruh, by some measures as accomplished and ambitious as O'Neill.

After Reagan's meeting with O'Neill, the president-elect's aides were furious at the speaker's condescension. Reagan, however, was amused. Never one to allow ego to get in the way of his objectives, he told me he thought it useful to be underestimated. This was vintage Reagan. He deliberately encouraged low estimates of his abilities with self-deprecating humor. When once asked what kind of governor he would be, he replied: "I don't know, I've never played a governor."

'ACTOR' DIDN'T MEAN 'AIRHEAD'

REAGAN, WHO HAD NEVER HELD POLITICAL OFFICE before he was elected governor, was undaunted by frequent observations that he lacked experience. Throughout his life he had talked his way into jobs for which he lacked formal qualification and done well at them. He had been a broadcaster, a movie actor, president of the Screen Actors Guild, a television host and a businessman. The professionals thought him too light—and the Democrats believed him too right—to succeed in politics. That was fine with Reagan.

The political community first took serious note of him when he delivered a rousing nationally televised speech for Barry Goldwater on Oct. 27, 1964, a week before Goldwater lost in a landslide to President Lyndon Johnson. Goldwater had been demonized as an "extremist," a label Democrats pinned on Reagan when he sought the California governorship in 1966. But it didn't stick with Reagan. Ordinary Californians knew him from movies in which he usually played a good guy—the "heartwarming role of himself," wrote author and historian Garry Wills—and from his years on television, notably as host of the long-running *General Electric Theater.*

In 1966 he had the name recognition, and two-term governor Edmund G. (Pat) Brown, who had routed Richard Nixon four years earlier, had the experience. Brown, a liberal Democrat, was proud of his reputation as a builder—of university campuses, of the nation's largest freeway network and of a mammoth aqueduct that carried water from the wetter northern part of the state to the parched, and rapidly growing, south. He had scars after eight years in office but was convinced he could win a third term if Republicans were foolish enough to nominate Reagan.

To help this happen, Brown authorized a smear of Reagan's primary opponent, George Christopher, a centrist former mayor of San Francisco. It backfired. Reagan easily won the primary, and Christopher united moderate Republicans behind him in the general election. Christopher told me years later that he might have sat out the election except for Brown's smear.

Brown had a blind spot. He regarded "actor" as a synonym for "airhead" and didn't realize that most Californians care more for Hollywood than for Sacramento. Brown said that while he had been doing great things for California, Reagan was being upstaged by a chimpanzee in the movie *Bedtime for Bonzo*. Late in the campaign, a Brown commercial showed the governor telling black schoolchildren that an actor shot Abraham Lincoln. Reagan defeated Brown by nearly a million votes.

THE PRACTICAL GOVERNOR

SWORN IN ON JAN. 2, 1967, Reagan faced a huge budget deficit. The state constitution required the budget to be balanced annually, but Brown's finance director had avoided a tax increase in 1966 with an unfunded changeover in state accounting methods. As a consequence, Reagan had nine months of revenues to pay for a year's spending.

Reagan promised in his inaugural address to "squeeze, cut and trim" the costs of government, but the shortfall he faced was beyond any cost control. So two days after he became governor he decided it was necessary to raise taxes, telling aides not to wait "until everyone forgets that we did not cause this problem, we only inherited it." This prompt decision surprised legislators, including state senator George Deukmejian, a future Republican governor of California who carried Reagan's tax bill. "A lot of people, including me, thought [Reagan] would be ideological,"

Actor? Politician?
What's the Difference?

A humorist weighs in as Reagan runs for governor

RONALD REAGAN WAS AND IS A VERY GOOD ACTOR, INDEED. Seventy-five percent of being a good actor is voice. Only a Spencer Tracy can get away with a squeaky, unheroic timbre and Ronald Reagan has such a strong, mellifluous delivery that he was once a sports announcer—and a good one at that.

Look at it this way: he had to be a good actor. He's not handsome. There's something earnest and unromantic about him. He couldn't make the gossip columns if he eloped with the Queen of Iran. He's got all that hair and teeth. His figure is good, but no one ever asked him to take off his shirt in a movie to help the box office. He never tested for Tarzan. He drinks sparingly. He lives within his budget: no solid-gold Lincolns or Cadillacs, no champagne parties in New York hotels. You color him grey. "Ronnie is like the end of autumn," a friend confides.

What he is, is a Republican. His reading runs to tomes on tax reform. His life is as organized as a monk's. He is a homebody. His marriage is one of those the fan magazines always hold up as paragons of matrimony.

But all the things Ronald Reagan is not as an actor, he is as a politician. As a fifty-four-year-old candidate, he is handsome. He is compelling, romantic even. If you're a forty-year-old female precinct worker, Ronald Reagan is an event in your life.

—Jim Murray, Esquire *magazine*
February 1966

The late Jim Murray was a Pulitzer Prize–winning columnist for the Los Angeles Times *from 1961 to 1998.*

Deukmejian told me in a 2002 interview. "We learned quickly that he was very practical."

The tax bill and the budget measure that accompanied it took seven months and many legislative turns and twists to enact. When it finally became law, it carried a price tag of $1 billion (nearly $7 billion in 2014 dollars), making it the largest tax increase ever enacted in any state up to that time. Using a formula devised mostly by Unruh's Democrats, it was a progressive bill that raised income-tax rates on the wealthy and on banks, corporations and insurance companies, while providing property-tax relief for older and low-income Californians.

The immediate consequence of the tax increase was that it stamped Reagan as a skillful politician in the eyes of the public and the Legislature. Its long-term effect as the economy improved in the late 1960s was that it provided more revenues than needed to erase the budget deficit. With the state awash in money, Reagan was able to maintain generous levels of spending for a myriad of public programs—even higher education, which he had targeted for cuts.

He was in a protracted struggle with the University of California and, to a lesser degree, with the state college (now state university) system over tuition and other issues. At the same time, he was embroiled in a very public and often emotional attempt to crack down on volatile student demonstrations against his policies and the Vietnam War. In the first weeks of his governorship Reagan had riled educators and students by proposing significant cuts in the budgets of both higher-education systems. The tax increase enabled him to restore most of the reductions.

On other fronts he struggled during his early months in office as he learned that the real-life role of governor was more demanding than he had imagined. "We were novice amateurs," said Lyn Nofziger, the candid director of communications. One sign of this amateurism was Reagan's naive faith that corporate America would ride to California's fiscal rescue; he expected CEOs to drop what they were doing and invest heavily in the state. Because he waited for corporate help that never materialized, Reagan was slow to name a director of finance, the most important state post. His first three choices turned him down. The fourth, who accepted, was a consultant as inexperienced in state government as Reagan. He was in over his head and gone within a year. Reagan's first chief of staff left even sooner.

The governor was a delegator who needed a good team around him to be effective. The new finance director was Caspar Weinberger, a lawyer with a Harvard education and a command of fiscal issues. The new chief of staff was Reagan's soft-spoken cabinet secretary, William P. Clark. He restored order to the governor's office before leaving to become a judge; Reagan later appointed him to the California Supreme Court. Clark was succeeded by Edwin Meese III, and they all would later join President Reagan's cabinet.

Reagan was also fortunate in having Thomas C. Reed as his first appointments secretary. Reed had wanted to be chief of staff. When he didn't get the job, he volunteered to be appointments secretary with a stipulation that he stay for only 100 days. Although Reed was partisan, he was determined not to staff the Reagan administration with political hacks. He found competent people to head most state agencies. Norman (Ike) Livermore, a Sierra Club member and a lumberman, was a particularly outstanding choice as state resources director, a key post in environmentally sensitive California.

Largely because he followed Livermore's lead, Reagan compiled a surprisingly strong environmental record. In his campaign for governor, he had told a timber group: "A tree's a tree. How many more do you need to look at?" Acting on that dubious insight, he sided with the timber industry in opposing the creation of a national redwood park on California's north coast. But Livermore was seen by environmentalists and the industry alike as an honest man with a gift for compromise. The result was the 53,000-acre Redwood National Park, created by Congress by combining federal land, two state parks and other acreage purchased from lumber companies.

On other environmental issues Reagan needed little convincing. He signed laws that imposed tough water-quality and smog-control standards and preserved the state's dwindling number of wild rivers. He sided with Livermore against California's powerful water establishment and the Army Corps of Engineers, which wanted to build a dam on the middle fork of the Eel River. So concerned was he that the dam would flood the scenic Round Valley, he even turned down federal funds that would have paid for it.

In his second term Reagan helped block a long-sought federal highway through the Minarets region of the High Sierra that would have bisected the John Muir Trail. The governor, on horseback with assistants and packhorses in tow, rode several miles into the mountains to survey the route—and condemn it. He criticized the State Highway Commission for "its tendency to go by the rule of the shortest distance between two points, regardless of what scenic wonder must be destroyed."

Although many of these environmental actions were controversial, they paled in emotional intensity beside the abortion issue, which took center stage during the early months of Reagan's governorship. As on so many issues, California was in the forefront of the national debate on abortion. In 1967, six years before the U.S. Supreme Court issued its landmark ruling in *Roe v. Wade*, a soft-spoken Democratic state senator from Beverly Hills named Anthony Beilenson introduced the Therapeutic Abortion Act to reduce what he called the "barbarous" practice of backroom abortions. The issue broke on religious rather than partisan lines, with Catholics opposed to the proposal and almost everyone else in favor. A large majority of Republican legislators supported the Beilenson bill.

Reagan personally viewed abortion as the taking of a life, and he insisted on amendments that he had been told would reduce the scope of abortions. When Beilenson accepted them and the Legislature sent the bill to Reagan's desk, he couldn't decide what to do. His aides, as divided as the Legislature on religious lines, gave him conflicting recommendations. Reagan talked to Cardinal Francis McIntyre, who presented the church's case against abortion, and to his father-in-law, Loyal Davis, a surgeon who supported it.

After several days of indecision he reluctantly signed the bill—much to his later regret. A provision allowing abortions to preserve the mental health of the mother became a virtual blank check for the procedure.

More than 2 million abortions would be performed under the Therapeutic Abortion Act. When the scope of the bill was beginning to emerge in 1968, I asked Reagan about it. He observed that he had been governor for only four months when the bill reached his desk and said he would not have signed it had he been more experienced. He became an outspoken opponent of abortion, except to save the life of the mother or in cases of rape or incest.

A SURPRISING ALLIANCE ON WELFARE REFORM

REAGAN RAN FOR REELECTION IN 1970 against the longtime Democratic strongman Unruh. Reagan started out 20 points ahead in the polls, but Unruh waged a spirited, populist campaign in which he depicted himself as a champion of the middle class and Reagan as the tool of the rich. Reagan's winning margin from 1966 was cut in half; he won by half a million votes in a year when 11 other Republican governors were defeated.

He was now no longer a novice who looked on government as an automatic enemy. During the closing stages of the campaign he was shaking hands at a rope line in working-class South Gate when a voice from the crowd asked, "When are you going to clean up politics?" The Reagan of 1966 likely would have agreed with the premise of the question. But in 1970 he responded, "Politics is far more honest than you think."

This insight led to a different approach in his second term as governor. Unruh was replaced as Assembly speaker by Bob Moretti, a young, energetic Democrat from Los Angeles who wanted to be governor someday and knew he needed to compile a record on which to run.

Welfare was the issue of the day. Aid to Families with Dependent Children (AFDC), a program that was federally mandated but with benefits set by the states, had been created by the Social Security Act of 1935 to assist children whose fathers were disabled or had abandoned their families. For decades it was a minor program. But as court decisions, executive rulings and legislative actions relaxed eligibility requirements, AFDC grew rapidly during the 1960s, prompting cutbacks in many states. In 1963 California had 375,000 AFDC recipients. By December 1969 the number was 1,150,000. A year later, a month after Reagan's reelection, 1,566,000 people were on the AFDC rolls—nearly one in every 13 Californians—and the caseload was increasing by 40,000 a month.

Meese had organized a welfare task force even before Reagan was reelected. Armed with its recommendations, the governor proposed legislation to restrict the caseload by cracking down on fraud and adding work requirements for welfare recipients. The bill also increased payments to the poorest recipients, who had not seen a hike in well over a decade.

Opposing Reagan's bill, Democrats contended that the caseload increase was the fault of hard economic times, even though caseloads had risen through good times and bad. The bill was stalled in committee for months while the two sides dueled by press release. Seeking to break the impasse, aides to the speaker and the governor suggested they meet privately. Reagan jumped at the chance. He trusted his negotiating skills, which he'd honed as president of the Screen Actors Guild. Moretti was also open-minded—and unafraid to negotiate. The two men rolled up their sleeves and pounded out a bill. In the process, as Moretti later said, he and the governor developed a "grudging respect" for each other.

The final version of the California Welfare Reform Act of 1971 (CWRA) was a complex measure that preserved the original goals of reducing fraud and increasing payments for the poorest recipients. Welfare rolls began declining immediately, falling by nearly 300,000 in three years. Democrats attributed this to improvement in the economy, but that wasn't the entire story. A thoughtful study by Frank Levy of the Urban League, no fan of Reagan, called the CWRA "a one-in-a-thousand policy success" that saved money and helped more recipients than it hurt. Levy estimated that the rolls had declined by 6% more than they would have without the Reagan reform.

Reagan and Moretti parlayed their cooperation on welfare reform into agreements on taxes and school financing. The governor also backed a program for early-childhood development and a master plan for education put forward by Wilson Riles, a progressive Democrat who was state superintendent of public instruction. "We did not go backward on education under Reagan's regime," Riles said. "We went forward."

Reagan and Moretti fell out in 1973 on a tax-limitation initiative that the governor advocated and the speaker opposed. It was rejected by the voters. Nonetheless, the cooperation of the governor and the speaker in much of the second term forged a record of achievement.

On balance, Ronald Reagan was a successful governor. Gifted as a politician, he had applied himself and learned on the job how to compromise while still advancing his agenda. He would be a better president because of this training. Although Tip O'Neill didn't know it the day he met the president-elect, California had taught Reagan how to hit major-league pitching.

Letters

Reagan writes about issues facing California

'THE RIGHT TO BE WRONG'

Sept. 15, 1965, to a woman who accused him of coddling right-wingers

[THE JOHN BIRCH SOCIETY] DOES NOT ENDORSE political candidates and even if it did I would not seek its endorsement any more than I would appeal to any "block," groups, clubs, etc. I intend to state my philosophy, my beliefs and my approach to current problems with the hope that individual voters will subscribe to those views and support me. In that case they will be buying my philosophy—I'm not buying theirs....

My refusal to indict this group has nothing to do with fence sitting but is because of my deep seated conviction that the greatness of our nation is our willingness to grant people the right to be wrong—so long as they do not infringe on the constitutional rights of others.

NOT A CASE OF AN 'EYE FOR AN EYE'

After January 1967, to a constituent who asked about the death penalty

LET ME SAY FIRST WITH REGARD to my mental attitude, as you put it, I certainly feel no hatred nor is my position on capital punishment motivated by some "eye for an eye" concept. It is true I believe we must retain capital punishment, and I believe there is backing for this in the Scriptures. However, this must be thought of in the light of a preventive to murder.

On my desk is a list of 12 murderers who were sentenced to prison and subsequently, having served their sentences, were released. They went on to murder 22 more victims.

As governor, I cannot put my personal feelings above the law. If our system of justice, including all the courts of appeal, decree a man must die for a crime, I can only reverse that decision if evidence is presented later which indicated he is entitled to clemency.

Believe me, no part of a governor's job is approached more prayerfully than this one.

'ONE BRIGHT MOMENT'

Oct. 23, 1968, to a student's father after antiwar demonstrations at the University of California, Santa Cruz

THERE IS NO NEED FOR ME TO GO INTO the sad experience of seeing students on that beautiful campus rioting, threatening physical harm to the regents assembled there, and cursing the regents with profanity and unrepeatable obscenities. Enough to say—it happened.

But out of all this came one bright moment, at least for me. On the bus tour of the campus, students had been assigned to the busses as guides. I found myself seated beside one of the nicest, most ladylike young women one could hope to meet— your daughter. After hearing her good common-sense reaction to all that was going on, I finally had to ask how she had been able to maintain such a sense of values in the atmosphere so prevalent there. She stated very simply, "That's the way my mother and father raised me."

You must be very proud and you have every right to be.

'YOU FACED THEM DOWN'

Jan. 4, 1971, to Sam Hayakawa, the president of San Francisco State University during a time of student unrest

I KNOW I SHOULDN'T DO THIS but can't resist being an "I told you so." Do you remember our phone conversation one morning during those dark days of battle [during student riots]? You were tired and understandably so and you asked, "when will it end?" I said, "it is ending, you are winning and while you can't see it now, one of these days it will be gone. It will just fade away." Well it has. But it faded away because you faced them down. Do you know where we can get another dozen like you?

'I UNDERSTAND POVERTY VERY WELL'

Circa 1974–75, to a woman questioning his commitment to public education when her program was not funded

IN 1971-1972 WE APPROPRIATED $41.6 MILLION for child development programs designed to serve preschool age children. In the current budget this has grown to $93.4 million. The program has more than doubled in three years.

I can well understand your position and your disappointment at not being funded. I hope you can understand mine.

You made a reference to movie actors and to the children of the poor people and it seemed to me the inference was that I lacked understanding of the problems of poverty. If I'm wrong I beg your pardon. If not let me assure you I understand poverty very well and from personal experience. I grew up in poverty and know full well how blessed I have been. Between us perhaps one day we can bring our society a little closer to ending poverty.

WELFARE FOR 'THOSE WHO TRULY NEEDED HELP'

After January 1975, to a woman asking about welfare reform and race

I AM AWARE THAT A CAMPAIGN has been waged to portray me as against the poor and the black.... First of all, our welfare reforms did not deny help to any deserving person. As much as anything they were designed to enable us to do more for those who truly needed help. California's welfare load was so widespread that the state hadn't been able to meet the increased cost of living. There had been no increase in the grants from 1958 to 1971. We increased the grants by 43 percent. The people we took off the rolls were not particularly Negroes—quite the contrary. We found for example one county in which 194 county employees—mainly white—were drawing welfare too.

In my eight years more Negroes were appointed to executive and policymaking positions in state government than had been appointed by all the previous California governors put together. You are absolutely right that our job is getting our story across.

'I DID NOT DYE MY HAIR'

May 5, 1979, to a columnist who questioned his effectiveness as governor
WHEN I TOOK OFFICE, California was insolvent and spending a million dollars a day more than tax revenues. In the eight years of our administration, we made the state solvent, attained a triple-A rating (Moody's) for California bonds and left the new governor a half-billion dollar surplus. We also returned $5.7 billion to the taxpayers in direct rebates and credits....

We increased support for public schools eight times as much as the increase in enrollment and increased the scholarship fund for needy students by 9,000 percent. While reducing the cost of welfare $2 billion in three years, we raised, at the same time, the grants for the needy by 43 percent....

One last point. You'll be pleased to know that a number of your colleagues (members of the capital press corps) made a number of trips to the barbershop where my hair was cut and discovered for themselves that I did not dye my hair. Now, happily, enough grey is showing to make such research unnecessary.

The Great Communicator

A SCRIPT AUTHENTIC TO HIMSELF

BY LANDON PARVIN

*Landon Parvin, who still advises political candidates, served
as a speechwriter for President Reagan, Presidents George H.W. Bush
and George W. Bush and California governor Arnold Schwarzenegger.*

T HE DECADE OF THE 1970S WAS NOT A GOOD ONE for American presidents. The first, politically corrupt, was forced from office because of his lies and deceptions. The second was an able caretaker but lacked eloquence and carried the burden of being appointed by a devious predecessor. And the third, Jimmy Carter, was an honest man but a micromanager who seemed powerless in the face of gas shortages, double-digit inflation, double-digit unemployment, a declining economy and the ignominy of having 52 Americans held hostage in Iran and terrorized for 444 days. Carter said the nation's problems were deeper than gas shortages, inflation or recession. The real threat, he said in a speech on July 15, 1979, was that Americans faced "a crisis of confidence."

And then came Ronald Reagan, the man who let America believe in itself again. In announcing his candidacy four months after Carter's speech, Reagan said the crisis the nation faced was not a failure of America's spirit; the failure was in its leaders. He insisted there was absolutely nothing wrong with the American people. After years of hand-wringing in Washington, his determination was a tonic—and was expressed with clarity: "I don't agree that our nation must resign itself to inevitable decline, yielding its proud position to other hands. I am totally unwilling to see this country fail in its obligations to itself and to other free peoples in the world." His optimism was not only sincere, it was infectious.

If Jimmy Carter projected a crisis of confidence, Ronald Reagan projected confidence itself, not just through his words but also through his unspoken manner—both of which contributed to his ability to communicate and lead.

First, even though my job as speechwriter to Reagan was to focus on words, let me say something about the power of the unspoken perception, because I think it was crucial to his leadership. During his presidency, two White House photos were particularly popular. One was of Reagan in a hammock at his ranch looking tanned and confident in a light blue work shirt and cowboy hat. The other was a photo of him in a tuxedo holding a glass of champagne raised in a toast. From these photos, you could see the comfort that flowed from his personality and the ease that came from his style, which in turn reassured people. The perception that he was at ease in his own skin gave people confidence in his leadership; it established trust that an adult was in charge and everything was going to be OK. Even when things didn't go so well or he made a mistake, and he temporarily paid a price in the polls, most people eventually gave him the benefit of the doubt because they were reassured by his basic character and nature.

I remember a memorial service that the president and Mrs. Reagan attended for 37 seamen who were killed on the U.S.S. *Stark* when an Iraqi jet fired on it in 1987. At the end of the ceremony, as the Navy Hymn played in the background, the president and his wife went from row to row and from family to family to express their condolences. At one point, he came to a young girl who looked to be about 3 and who was being held by a man I assumed to be her uncle. The president paused, and the man explained something to him. You could tell he was saying that the girl was the daughter of one of the seamen who had been killed. The president, whose face already carried great sadness, looked even more grief-stricken. He walked a couple of steps beyond the girl to the next family but then turned back to look at her once again with the most unmistakably pained expression on his face.

What the Great Communicator communicated with his anguish for the little girl—as he did with the snap of a salute that he routinely gave the Marine at the bottom of the stairs as he stepped off Marine One—was that he could be trusted not to send America's men and women in uniform into harm's way unless he felt the greater good of the nation was at stake. What the camera caught was the true character of Ronald Reagan, which buttressed his leadership. He had a presidential presence that conveyed strength and confidence. He would never have even considered delivering an evening address to the nation wearing a sweater, as his predecessor had done. I believe this strong and honest presence helped build the foundation of the Great Communicator before he ever spoke a word.

As for the words, you frequently hear that Reagan earned the title of the Great Communicator because he was an actor and could deliver a line. While he himself said his acting skills were invaluable, good actors don't necessarily make good politicians. How Reagan the actor helped Reagan the leader was that he knew you had to be comfortable in your role and you had to have something meaningful to say. Reagan's presidential role and script were authentic to him.

Goethe wrote, "When ideas fail, words come in very handy." Today, that is certainly the case for most political speeches from either party—harsh drivel without the benefit of substantive thought. But Reagan genuinely had something to say. In his farewell address to the nation, he said he wasn't a great communicator, but in fact he communicated great things.

He advocated cutting taxes, restoring our economy through free enterprise, controlling the size of government, returning power to the states, rebuilding our defenses—and he explained the principles behind them. He may not have accomplished all of these goals, but he made them central issues in American politics. With the exception of rebuilding our defenses, they are still central.

This being in the days before social media, Reagan believed that it took 20 years of speaking about an issue before it began to sink into the public consciousness. He felt one of the roles of a leader was to educate. In fact, it was an essential duty of a leader, because how else could you move the public from point A to point B? Reagan had ideas he wanted to bring to the attention of the American people, ideas he had been speaking about for nearly 30 years before he was elected president.

Take That, Big Government

Reagan makes his point with humor

"I am not worried about the deficit. It is big enough to take care of itself."

"Politics is supposed to be the second-oldest profession. I have come to realize that it bears a very close resemblance to the first."

"The nine most terrifying words in the English language are: 'I'm from the government and I'm here to help.'"

"Politics is not a bad profession. If you succeed, there are many rewards. If you disgrace yourself, you can always write a book."

"One way to make sure crime doesn't pay would be to let the government run it."

"I have wondered at times what the Ten Commandments would have looked like if Moses had run them through the U.S. Congress."

"Government is like a baby. An alimentary canal with a big appetite at one end and no sense of responsibility at the other."

"A taxpayer is someone who works for the federal government but doesn't have to take a civil service exam."

"I'm afraid I can't use a mule. I have several hundred up on Capitol Hill."

"Government's view of the economy could be summed up in a few short phrases: If it moves, tax it. If it keeps moving, regulate it. And if it stops moving, subsidize it."

I have helped a number of political candidates over the years, and you would be surprised how many think all they need to do is to mindlessly spout buzzwords and applause lines. But without substance, even the best lines quickly lose their force. Reagan loved arguments based on political thought and philosophy. This is largely lost in today's politics.

Another vital force behind his words was his determination. He told me when I was helping him put together a book of his speeches that the impact of a speech most often results not from how eloquently you say something but from the meaning and clarity of the words. This was certainly the case early on in his administration when he fired the nation's air-traffic controllers after they violated the law and their own oaths and went out on strike.

On the steps of the Rose Garden that August morning, the president was plainspoken: "I must tell those who fail to report for duty this morning they are in violation of the law, and if they do not report for work within 48 hours, they have forfeited their jobs and will be terminated." Those words had force behind them. No moving red lines. No poetic passages. And in 48 hours the striking controllers were terminated. We now know that the Soviets were impressed by this resolve, and it influenced their measure of the president. It took years for the air-traffic system to return to normal, but in the president's mind, as he said, "the principle was worth the price."

Finally, I believe one other thing in particular helped him become known as the Great Communicator. He understood the power of articulating the unarticulated truth. We were still in the midst of the Cold War with the Soviet Union when Reagan began his presidency. He denounced this regime, which had purposely starved millions of its own people during Stalin's time, as an evil empire. He said it would end up on the "ash heap" of history. And he gave voice to another truth that no major leader had ever uttered despite the simplicity of its logic: "Mr. Gorbachev, tear down this wall!" That sentence reverberated around the world.

When he ran against Jimmy Carter in 1980, he highlighted a devastatingly uncomplicated truth in a question he asked the American people, which candidates have been using against incumbents ever since: "Are you better off today than you were four years ago?"

He at times gave voice to the politically incorrect or to what the average citizen believed, no matter how dismissive the media thought his words to be, as he did in a 1976 presidential-campaign speech expressing his opposition to ceding ownership of the Panama Canal to the Panamanian government: "We should end those negotiations on giving away the Panama Canal and tell General Torrijos—we bought it, we paid for it, we built it and we're going to keep it."

Is my thinking about Reagan skewed by my affection and respect for my old boss? I am sure that is the case, but I am not the only one who recognized his communication and leadership qualities—the lion's share of the American people did too. He won his first presidential election before he even got out of the shower to watch the evening's returns, and his second election was a landslide in which he won 49 of the 50 states.

He felt he was president of all the people whether they voted for him or not, and I will give you one final example. I was a young man, in my early 30s, when I went to work for Ronald Reagan. I would sometimes write lines that I knew were surefire applause lines. I always anticipated hearing my words excite the audience, but when the president delivered them he would usually downplay them, so that the Great Communicator would receive no applause on the line at all. I was always a little disappointed, and I would think, Why didn't he go for it? Didn't he see he could have hit it out of the park?

What I finally realized was that he purposely delivered the line in his genial, low-key way because otherwise it would have been too divisive or too rhetorical or too grand. He wanted to talk to the people, to educate them, to lead them, all of them. This was not about something personal, not something ego-driven, such as getting applause; this was about leading the nation. There is a reason, in my view, that there were Reagan Democrats but today there are no Obama Republicans.

I was asked the other day to share my assessment of Reagan's legacy as a communicator. As much as I hate to admit it, while his legacy lingered for a while, today it is pretty much gone. If you listen to the speeches of most politicians on the left and right, you will hear passages of sunny optimism, which are pure Ronald Reagan, but the words themselves are hollow. They rightfully link his success to his optimism, and so they know they, too, should be optimistic. But where is the authenticity when they are constantly at the throats of the other party and when every battle is a prelude to doomsday?

Where is the geniality of spirit that enabled Reagan to work with the other side? Where is the practical ideology that allowed him to reach across the aisle to get a deal? Where in today's leaders are the risks of leadership that Reagan took? Neither in their words nor their actions.

He was one of a kind, and I believe the nation was better for his presence in our lives. I am certainly better for his presence in mine.

Excerpts from Some of Reagan's Most Memorable Speeches

From national destiny and old age to tax vetoes and tyranny

"I, in my own mind, have always thought of America as a place in the divine scheme of things that was set aside as a promised land.... Any person with the courage, with the desire to tear up their roots, to strive for freedom, to attempt and dare to live in a strange and foreign place, to travel halfway across the world, was welcome here."
June 1952, commencement address at William Woods College

"You and I have a rendezvous with destiny. We will preserve for our children this, the last best hope of man on earth, or we will sentence them to take the first step into a thousand years of darkness.... We have the ability and the dignity and the right to make our own decisions."
Oct. 27, 1964, in support of GOP presidential candidate Barry Goldwater

"I'm convinced that today the majority of Americans want what those first Americans wanted: a better life for themselves and their children; a minimum of government authority. Very simply, they want to be left alone in peace and safety to take care of the family by earning an honest dollar and putting away some savings. This may not sound too exciting, but there is something magnificent about it. On the farm, on the street corner, in the factory and in the kitchen, millions of us ask nothing more, but certainly nothing less than to live our own lives according to our values—at peace with ourselves, our neighbors and the world."
July 6, 1976, televised address

"A recession is when your neighbor loses his job. A depression is when you lose yours. Recovery is when Jimmy Carter loses his."
Sept. 1, 1980, presidential campaign speech

"With regard to the freedom of the individual for choice with regard to abortion, there is one individual who is not being considered at all, and that's the one who is being aborted. And I have noticed that everybody that is for abortion has already been born."
Sept. 21, 1980, presidential debate

"Next Tuesday all of you will go to the polls, will stand there in the polling place and make a decision. I think when you make that decision, it might be well if you would ask yourself, are you better off than you were four years ago?"
Oct. 28, 1980, presidential debate

"In this present crisis, government is not the solution to our problem; government is the problem."
Jan. 20, 1981, inaugural address

"We don't have an option of living with inflation and its attendant tragedy.... We have an alternative, and that is the program for economic recovery. True, it'll take time for the favorable effects of our program to be felt. So we must begin now. The people are watching and waiting. They don't demand miracles. They do expect us to act. Let us act together."
Feb. 18, 1981, speaking to Congress

"It is the Soviet Union that runs against the tide of history.... [It is] the march of freedom and democracy which will leave Marxism-Leninism on the ash heap of history, as it has left other tyrannies which stifle the freedom and muzzle the self-expression of the people."
June 8, 1982, speaking to Britain's Parliament

"And make no mistake about it, this attack was not just against ourselves or the Republic of Korea. This was the Soviet Union against the world and the moral precepts which guide human relations among people everywhere. It was an act of barbarism, born of a society which wantonly disregards individual rights and the value of human life and seeks constantly to expand and dominate other nations."

Sept. 5, 1983, following the Soviet downing of a South Korean airliner

"My fellow Americans, I'm pleased to announce that I've signed legislation outlawing the Soviet Union. We begin bombing in five minutes."

Aug. 11, 1984, joking during a sound check before a radio broadcast

"I want you to know that also I will not make age an issue of this campaign. I am not going to exploit, for political purposes, my opponent's youth and inexperience."

Oct. 21, 1984, presidential debate with Walter Mondale

"I have my veto pen drawn and ready for any tax increase that Congress might even think of sending up. And I have only one thing to say to the tax increasers: 'Go ahead, make my day.'"

March 13, 1985

"The crew of the space shuttle *Challenger* honored us by the manner in which they lived their lives. We will never forget them, nor the last time we saw them—this morning, as they prepared for their journey, and waved goodbye, and 'slipped the surly bonds of earth' to 'touch the face of God.'"

Jan. 28, 1986, after the space shuttle Challenger *exploded*

"A few months ago, I told the American people I did not trade arms for hostages. My heart and my best intentions still tell me that's true, but the facts and the evidence tell me it is not."

March 4, 1987, admitting to the Tower Commission findings on the Iran-contra scandal

"General Secretary Gorbachev, if you seek peace, if you seek prosperity for the Soviet Union and Eastern Europe, if you seek liberalization: come here to this gate! Mr. Gorbachev, open this gate! Mr. Gorbachev, tear down this wall!"

June 12, 1987, at the Brandenburg Gate in Berlin

"I've spoken of the shining city all my political life.... And how stands the city on this winter night?... After 200 years, two centuries, she still stands strong and true on the granite ridge, and her glow has held steady no matter what storm. And she's still a beacon, still a magnet for all who must have freedom, for all the pilgrims from all the lost places who are hurtling through the darkness, toward home."

Jan. 11, 1989, farewell address

"I know in my heart that man is good. That what is right will always eventually triumph. And there's purpose and worth to each and every life."

Nov. 4, 1991, dedication of his presidential library

"I now begin the journey that will lead me into the sunset of my life. I know that for America there will always be a bright dawn ahead. Thank you, my friends. May God always bless you."

Nov. 5, 1994, letter announcing his Alzheimer's diagnosis

Reagan, with Nancy, campaigned nonstop in 1976 in a losing bid for the GOP presidential nomination.

In June 1980, the Reagans ride horseback through their 688-acre ranch, where he once engraved a rock with their initials inside a heart.

With his VP pick, George H.W. Bush, at his side, Reagan jokes with former president Ford at the 1980 GOP convention.

Nancy holds the family Bible while Chief Justice Warren Burger swears in President-elect Ronald Reagan on Jan. 20, 1981.

Longtime friends Frank Sinatra and the first lady were enjoying a dance at Reagan's 70th-birthday White House bash on Feb. 6, 1981, when the new commander in chief asked to cut in.

GET WELL SOON
Mr. President
Jim, Tim, and Tom

A giant get-well card helps ease the pain for Reagan, who was shot just 70 days into his first term.

Reagan and aide Michael Deaver (left) join chief of staff James Baker in November 1981 for a turkey hunt on Baker's Texas ranch.

Reagan (on Air Force One in 1982) didn't hesitate to tell reporters when he felt he had been misrepresented.

British Prime Minister Margaret Thatcher and Reagan (at a G-7 summit in Versailles in 1982) formed a close personal bond.

The Reagans attend the Nov. 4, 1983, Camp Lejeune memorial service for 260 service members killed in Lebanon and Grenada.

As time passed, Reagan (lunching in 1984 with Bush) gained increasing respect for his No. 2.

The 1986 nuclear-weapons summit between Reagan and Gorbachev in Reykjavik, Iceland, collapsed in a dispute over the U.S. Strategic Defense Initiative ("Star Wars") but laid the foundation for a later accord.

"No excuses," Reagan said in his 1987 televised address on the Iran-contra affair. "It was a mistake."

"Tear down this wall," Reagan, at West Berlin's Brandenburg Gate on June 12, 1987, told Gorbachev.

The president and first lady leave the Capitol on Jan. 20, 1989, his last day in office.

Remembering Reagan

FRIENDS AND COLLEAGUES RECALL THE LEADER AND THE MAN

GEN. COLIN POWELL, SEN. BOB DOLE,
SEN. JOHN MCCAIN, LORRAINE M. WAGNER
AND MICHAEL DEAVER

Gen. Colin Powell

'WE MUST NEVER, EVER USE NUCLEAR WEAPONS'

Colin Powell, national-security adviser under Reagan and later named the youngest-ever chairman of the Joint Chiefs of Staff, talks about his boss's trusting management style, his abiding respect for the military and his determination to lessen the threat of nuclear war.

ONE DAY WHILE I WAS NATIONAL-SECURITY adviser, I went into the Oval Office to brief the president on a very difficult situation I was working on. And the two of us are sitting in there alone; he's in the chair by the fireplace facing the windows, and I'm on the couch. I start talking about what's going on, and it's complicated, with the Department of State, Commerce, trade representatives, blah, blah, blah, having different positions.

But he's paying no attention to me. So I get a little disturbed. I try talking faster, then louder—nothing. He keeps looking over my shoulder out through the French doors toward the Rose Garden. And I'm wondering, "What the heck is going on here?"

Finally I run out of anything else to say, and he pops up and says, "Colin, Colin, look, the squirrels just came and got the nuts that I put out this morning." And I say, "Yes, Mr. President, I see." I wait a minute, then say, "Well, I better go now." I go back to my office and I sit there staring out the window wondering, "What the devil was that all about?"

Then it hits me, it's clear as a bell. What he was saying to me was, "Colin, you know I really love you, and I will sit here for as long as you want me to as you tell me about your problem. But until you give me a problem, I'm going to watch the squirrels in the Rose Garden." What he was essentially saying was, "I hired you to handle problems like this, I trust you and I've empowered you, and I have other things to worry about. And that's how I work."

There's a picture he signed for me of the two of us sitting by the fireplace, and he wrote, "Dear Colin, If you say it is so, it must be true." I mean, wow. I sometimes screwed up. But he trusted me. His philosophy was to get people he was confident in and then turn them loose.

Which doesn't for a second mean he avoided tough calls. There was a crisis in the Persian Gulf with us chasing some Iranian ships that had fired at us, and to continue the action we had to cross into Iranian territorial waters. Frank Carlucci is the secretary of defense, and he calls me and says we need immediate permission from the president to cross the line. I go down to the Oval Office, and the president is calmly sitting there autographing photographs even though there's a battle going on. But he figures the Pentagon can handle the situation. So I tell him the problem, he asks me a couple of questions, I answer them and he says, "Do it." Decisive. On the money.

He was always focusing on the things that a president should focus on—vision, keeping America strong. Did he have to make deals? Yes, sure. You can say we can't raise taxes, but he did raise taxes a half-dozen times. But he was always able to make tactical judgments because he was anchored in a broader vision that the American people understood and wanted.

Making the military strong was part of that. He started putting money into the Pentagon that, frankly, was unbelievable. President Carter started the funding, but it was really Reagan and Secretary of Defense Caspar Weinberger and then Carlucci who began to fix the Pentagon. We in the military at the time have never forgotten what they did to restore pride in the military. He made us feel worthy and deserving of praise.

And he wasn't strengthening the military for the purpose of fighting the Soviet Union, but for keeping the Soviet Union from ever thinking that they could win such a fight. What he really wanted to do was to get the Soviet Union to understand that there was a better world waiting for them. That's what he kept saying to Mikhail Gorbachev. He kept insisting, "Come visit us in California." He was dying to take that man to California—the Golden State.

He was willing to listen to the Russians. In the first years of his administration the Soviet leaders were dying one after the other. Reagan used to say, "I'll talk to them if they would live long enough." Then along came Gorbachev, a young guy who understood the problems that the Soviet Union had.

Reagan was always a little bit above the rest of us. Sometimes it got him in trouble. But he had a broader understanding of the long-term goals and a magic connection to the American people. That's why he was ultimately so successful—even with some setbacks. He always had that shining-city-on-the-hill vision, and that determination that we were going to be strong and we were going to help the Soviet Union get out of the problems they had.

He believed to the depths of his heart that we must never, ever use nuclear weapons. He was antinuclear to the point that we sometimes had to caution him about looking too eager to negotiate over our arsenal. Margaret Thatcher used to scratch her head and ask, "Will he really get rid of all of them?" He would have if he could.

Sen.
Bob Dole

'HE COULD CONVERSE WITH ANYBODY'

Bob Dole became chairman of the Senate Committee on Finance when
Reagan took office and worked closely with the president on tax reform.
He recalls how Reagan demonstrated leadership above management skills,
and handicaps the former president's prospects if he could run today.

REAGAN WASN'T A HARD-LINE KIND OF POLITICIAN. When we would work on complicated legislation, he'd tell me, "Get me 70 or 80%, and we'll get the rest next year," which demonstrated that he wasn't a rigid ideologue. He knew that we had to compromise sometimes and that he couldn't get everything he sent to Congress.

And he got along with Congress, got acquainted with them. That's one thing President Obama has failed to do. Reagan had this personality; you couldn't dislike him. You might not agree with him, but few people would dislike him. And he never seemed to be perturbed.

He'd greet congressional members when they came to the White House, shaking hands with everybody. He made them feel like he really knew them, even though he didn't always. Sometimes he'd tell a story. He was always on time. He was scripted most of the time, but we always had a productive meeting with him.

I'd get a letter from Reagan after a bill passed the committee thanking me for my leadership. He probably had someone write them, but he always signed them, and it's nice to get recognized by the president for what you've done.

I remember one time him coming to the Capitol to see a Republican senator to try to get his vote on a bill. It was Steve Symms from Idaho, and I told the White House before Reagan came up that he was not going to be successful. But the White House said the president was going to try it anyway. So he came to the Capitol and met with Steve Symms for about 30 minutes, and Steve said, "I just can't do it." So the president walked out, went back to the White House disappointed, but he didn't rail against Symms. He had tried to reason with him, he didn't succeed, he moved on.

There was one time he got mad. We had passed a bill creating withholding taxes on interest and dividends, and the bankers were up in arms. When Reagan heard their complaints, he threw his glasses down on the table and said, "Those so-and-so's." He was mad, but it was clear that he was going to defend the bill and not cave in to the pressure. And the bill passed.

Reagan had the edge when it came to convincing someone that they ought to do this or do that. George H.W. Bush was good at that, too, because he'd been in the House of Representatives and he knew a lot of the Republicans, but he didn't quite have the star power that Reagan had. Or the popularity.

Here Reagan was in the White House, but he could converse with anybody, regardless of their status. He left that impression with the working people. He got a good chunk of union members to vote for him, even though the union leaders were against him.

Even when he was tough and fired the air-traffic controllers after they went on strike, the people liked him. That's another hallmark of the Reagan administration; he took an action that was the correct thing to do, and the American people were with him. That strike was early in his administration, but he fired those people, and that showed leadership. Not management, but leadership—and a lot of political courage.

I had a rare disagreement with him when I ran for president in '88 against Bush. I won the caucuses in Iowa and we were all campaigning in New Hampshire, and Bush arranged for a meeting with President Reagan. The media showed them at lunch together, which I think gave Bush what he needed to carry New Hampshire. I can understand—Bush was the vice president, and I assume he had a close relationship with Reagan. But I was a leader in the Senate trying to get things done for the president, so I was more than a little disappointed.

People still on Capitol Hill and in commentary bring up the Reagan era as the golden years for the Republican Party. I agree. He was able to uplift the country and give hope to everyone. And he was a traditional conservative.

I don't know how he'd compare to today's conservatives. He might not be far enough right to satisfy some, but I think he could still win the election. The people are generally center-left or center-right—and that's where Reagan drilled for votes.

He was a great president, a good American and just a good man. What you saw is what you got.

Sen. John McCain

'HE NEVER BETRAYED HIS PRINCIPLES'

Shot down over Vietnam during a bombing mission in 1967, John McCain was held prisoner until 1973. Inspired by Reagan and the then-governor's concern for the POWs, he ran for office in 1981. He was equally moved years later by the poise the ailing Reagan showed at one of their last meetings.

W HEN RONALD REAGAN WAS GOVERNOR OF California, about the only thing that united our very fractured country over the war in Vietnam was the concern for the American prisoners in Hanoi. Many of the Navy and Air Force pilots were based out of the West Coast, and one day Reagan met in his office in Sacramento with some families of the POWs to talk about what should be done to bring those POWs home. As he started to speak, a little boy walked up and tugged on his sleeve. The governor leaned down, the little boy said something, and the governor took the boy out of his office and down the hall. Well, the little boy had to go to the bathroom.

When they came out, the governor said he hadn't performed that chore in quite a few years, then began his statement again. This little boy was still standing there; his name was Todd Hanson, and his father was Marine Maj. Stephen Paul Hanson, who had been shot down just a few months earlier. The boy tugged on the governor's sleeve again and said, "Will you please help bring my daddy home?" From that time until the POWs came home, Reagan wore a bracelet with Major Hanson's name on it.

Unfortunately, Major Hanson was not one of those who came back alive. But Reagan and Nancy became very emotionally involved in the POW-MIA issue, and when the POWs finally did come home, we were invited to a reception in California sponsored by the Reagans. That was when I first met them. I was invited to their house in Sacramento one evening, and we spent an hour or so together. I was inspired by him, by his example; that was one of the factors that led me to run for public office.

He had a very personal commitment to the people he served— and to the principles he believed in. He was able to turn Barry Goldwater's conservative principles into a political movement that would one day gain the support of the majority of Americans. That took some doing. After the 1964 election, I don't think there were many political pundits who thought that conservatives would ever make a comeback.

But Reagan went on to hone a viable conservative approach to issues like national security, big government and lower taxes. He also got things done; he had an ability to marshal his own troops, but he also knew he had to reach across the aisle. He and Democratic House Speaker Tip O'Neill developed a personal relationship that allowed them to work closely together. And I don't mean to take a shot at President Obama, or even President Bush, George W., but Reagan sat down with the other side and worked out agreements.

There's a story that Tip O'Neill was talking to his conference, and a couple of the Democrats stood up and said, "Why do you spend all that time with Reagan? We don't like it." And Tip O'Neill said, "I'll tell you why, it's because I like him."

Of course that doesn't mean there weren't bitter fights. I remember the Iran-contra affair—there was some bitter fighting, bitter and angry. But the beauty of Ronald Reagan—and it's something future presidents and this president should really learn from—is that when he finally understood the extent of the scandal, he went on national television and said, "I was wrong, I was responsible." The American people watched him, accepted what he said and moved on.

If you believe that all presidents are responsible for what happens on their watch, then Lebanon was also a failing. The barracks bombing in Beirut was one of the early manifestations of the kind of terrorism that we have grown accustomed to today. But then, it was shocking to the American public, it was terribly tragic, and the circumstances of how the bomber got through security so easily are shameful. The Marine guards didn't have any rounds in the chambers of their guns. It's bizarre. But right after the bombing, the revulsion of the American people was clear. If Reagan hadn't pulled the troops out, Congress would have forced him to.

But in that era, foreign policy was really all about the Cold War and the Soviet Union. The Middle East was ancillary. Terrible things did happen there, but overall, I would argue that, in the words of Margaret Thatcher, "Reagan won the Cold War without firing a shot." That's his legacy.

At the end of the day, I would say that Ronald Reagan would compromise for the purpose of achieving a beneficial result, but, to my knowledge, he never betrayed or compromised his principles.

One of the last times I saw him was long after he had retired, and he was suffering from Alzheimer's and his health was not good, and I was asked to introduce him at a fundraiser for the Fisher House Foundation that was being held on the U.S.S. *Intrepid* in New York Harbor. There weren't a lot of people, but it was a very worthy cause; Fisher Houses give free temporary housing to military and veterans' families while a loved one gets medical treatment. It was pretty obvious that this terrible disease had taken its toll on Reagan. We sat together, about eight people at this table, and he didn't really say a lot during the dinner. But then it came time for him to make remarks. He got up to the podium, with the teleprompter in front of him, and he gave an absolutely pitch-perfect speech of about 15 minutes. After he finished, he came down from the stage and was just as he had been before he stood at the podium. It was a remarkable thing to witness. He had a gift.

Lorraine M. Wagner

A WHITE DINNER JACKET COVERED WITH LIPSTICK

*What began in 1943 with a Reagan fan note from 13-year-old
Philadelphian Lorraine Makler grew into a 51-year friendship. She
received nearly 200 personal letters from Reagan. Here, she recalls the time
she spent in Dixon, Ill., with Reagan and his mother in the summer of 1950.*

I N MAY 1950 RON'S MOM, NELLE, WROTE ME AND SAID
he was coming to Philadelphia for a U.S. Savings Bond
drive, so I went down to see him in Independence Square,
and he gave me a beautiful smile and shook my hand. I
was ecstatic. I thought that was the pinnacle, meeting a
movie actor. I told him I had heard from his mother that he was
going to be honored at Dixon's annual summer celebration, which
was several days of parades and gatherings. Fan-club president
Zelda Multz and I had already made plans to go. Ron said, "Oh,
you'll love Dixon!"

Ron led the first parade mounted on a palomino; horses were
his great love. About 600 other riders followed him down Galena
Avenue into the business district. The streets were lined with
thousands of Dixonites and visitors. After the parade there was
a buffet lunch at the state-hospital grounds.

As soon as Ron dismounted, we gathered with him to take
a few pictures, but Zelda forgot to unlock the camera, so there
were a few ill-at-ease moments as we waited for her to fix it. But

Ron picked up on this right away and broke into some hilarious story, and we all started laughing. The shutter was released, and so was the tension.

Ron was exceedingly perceptive. Three years earlier, I had spoken to him on the phone when he was at his home in Los Angeles. He had just been discharged from the hospital after a near-death experience with viral pneumonia; about that same time a child with Jane Wyman was born prematurely and had died 12 hours later. I was struggling to find the right words to acknowledge that tragedy, but I was only 18 and all I finally came out with was, "I don't like knowing what I know." He was the one suffering, yet his first thought was to rescue me from my awkwardness. "Thank you," he said. "I understand."

When we finished taking pictures after the parade in Dixon, Moms Nelle insisted we sit at the VIP table with her and Ron and Mrs. Walgreen, the one from the Walgreens drugstore chain. We were stunned when Mrs. Walgreen invited us to stay at her estate outside Dixon with Ron and Nelle.

At the end of each night, Ron would go out with old friends, and the next morning at breakfast Moms would ask, "What time did you get in? Mrs. Walgreen left the light on for you all night!" He just smiled and went on to the next subject. One morning the phone rang, and he came back into the room and told us he had gotten the lead role in *Bedtime for Bonzo*. He laughed and said, "The monkey has the best part."

On the first night of the Dixon festivities, the local theater premiered *Louisa*, Ron's latest movie. Zelda and I were asked to introduce Ron after his mother spoke. Moms Nelle was a magnificently warm, articulate woman who often ended sentences with "Dontcha know?" Everybody says Ron's ability as a raconteur came from his father, but he got some from her as well. She could tell a story, and she could go on. So before the second showing, Ron collared me and said, "I don't care what you say or how you do it, but please get my mother off that stage. Don't let her keep talking about me!"

The next night at the Masonic Temple Hall he gave an amazing speech. He had no cards, no notes; there was no such thing as a teleprompter. He talked about what it meant to be a poor boy growing up in a small town and how he felt nothing but gratitude for what America had given him. At this time he was still focused on his acting career, well before he was soliciting votes, so it was from his heart. Two more minutes of listening to him, I'd have grabbed a flag and gotten up on the roof.

On several occasions during our visit, Moms Nelle said she hoped Ron would dance with her. That meant a lot to her. She wrote a few times to say she had been having horrible headaches and wasn't sure if she was going to get to Dixon. She was not well and didn't know how much time she had left. Ron said he wanted to dance with her, but he was still limping from a serious broken leg and was concerned that he wouldn't be able to escape a rush on the dance floor.

If you had any doubt about the fervor that the people of Dixon felt for him, you just had to see his beautiful white dinner jacket at the end of the night, covered with hand prints and lipstick marks. Finally Ron got up and said, "Let's go, Nelle." She was so excited that afterward when we left in the convertible to go back to Mrs. Walgreen's, Nelle climbed onto the top of the back seat like you do in a parade. Ron was about to go off with friends, but he was so concerned about her that he kept saying to me, "Hold her in! Hold her in!" He didn't leave until he knew she was safe.

Michael Deaver

'THERE WAS AN AURA ABOUT HIM'

*Michael Deaver was a close adviser throughout Reagan's political life.
In this excerpt from 2001's* A Different Drummer, *he recalls his first
sighting of Reagan and his last visit with the former president.
On Deaver's death from pancreatic cancer in 2007 at age 69, Nancy Reagan
said he was "the closest of friends to both Ronnie and me."*

I HAD SEEN REAGAN FOR THE FIRST TIME A YEAR EARLIER, in 1964, in the lobby of the Ambassador Hotel in downtown Los Angeles. I was just another faceless twenty-something back in those days, working quietly within the bowels of the California Republican Party while we all tried to recover from Barry Goldwater's recent slaughter at the polls. I had been lured into the party by the Arizona senator's straight talk, his promise to do the right thing and implement a real conservative agenda.

The Ambassador event was just another in a seemingly endless stream of political fund-raisers, speeches, and grip-and-grin sessions; but the lobby was full. The doors to my left swung open and Ronald Wilson Reagan walked into the lobby unescorted....

I had grown up stargazing in Southern California, I knew my stuff. I could pick out an actor when I saw one, and I was seeing one now. This guy looked like Hollywood incarnate. Everything was too perfect: the flawless hair, that robust chest, those rosy cheeks. I was sure he was wearing makeup. His walk was practiced and perfected—the only thing missing was the book on his head. Of course, I'd heard about this Ronald Reagan fellow. I knew his movies, vaguely, and I'd seen him hosting *Death Valley Days* and *GE Theater*. Word was that he could deliver some good zingers on the rubber-chicken circuit. In my book none of that added up to much of a political future, but I must say, looking back over all those years, that there was an aura about him even then. And somebody, after all, would have to lead the party out of the ruins of the Goldwater debacle.

REAGAN DECIDES TO RUN FOR PRESIDENT

I WAS WITH HIM NOT ONLY WHEN the election returns came in, but also at the precise moment he decided that he wanted the big job. With Reagan, there were no senior staff meetings to discuss such stuff, no trial balloons floated on the evening news to gauge the public's interest. Sure, there had been countless meetings where Reagan would listen, but he never said, "I'm running" until we were sitting together on an airplane in early 1976. Reagan had left the governor's mansion just two years earlier, and he'd been wowing conservative groups across the country with The Speech ever since. We had just taken our seats on a flight from Los Angeles to San Francisco when an attractive woman he had never met before knelt in the aisle next to his seat. "Governor," she said, "you must run for president. You must do it for the people who believe in the things you do."

I laughed to myself. I had seen it a million times before. Reagan would grin and shake her hand, thank her, and maybe sign an autograph if asked. This time, though, he just nodded and told her to have a good day. After she took her seat a couple of rows behind us, Reagan looked to see if she was out of hearing range. "You know, she's right," he said in a hushed tone. "I don't think Jerry Ford can win, and if I don't run, I'm going to be like the guy who always sat on the bench and never got in the game."...

I listened for the next hour as he went over the pros and cons of taking the plunge. Ten different men would probably

cite ten different reasons to run for president, but Reagan simply knew that he could, unlike Ford or Nixon, connect with the
people. This was the key, he said. He didn't use sophisticated
polling or do an Electoral College breakdown. He didn't care if
he lined up all the GOP governors, senators, or congressmen or
how much money he'd have to find to run a national campaign.
I think he just believed in his heart that he was the right guy at
the right time.

Toward the end of that memorable flight he explained, "Mike,
I remember in the movie *Santa Fe Trail*, I played George Custer as
a young lieutenant. The dying captain said to me, 'You have got
to take over.' And my line was 'I can't, I can't.' And the captain
said 'You must, it's your duty.' That's the way I feel about this,
it's my duty," he said, "I have to run. I'm going to run." Reagan
would often use movies as ways to illustrate his logic. To me this
made perfect sense—that's the world he knew—but I also knew
this time that he was dead serious.

INAUGURATION DAY, AND A CLEAN SLATE

THE MORNING OF THE TRANSFER OF POWER, the traditional
swearing in on the steps of the U.S. Capitol, I arrived at Blair
House at 8:00 a.m. sharp to greet the Reagans. On my way over,
I assumed that the president-elect would be practicing the most
important speech of his life. I walked in and greeted Nancy.

"Where's the governor?" I asked.

Careful not to disrupt the labors of her stylist, Nancy moved
only her mouth, saying, "I guess he's still in bed."

I didn't believe it.... I checked for myself, cracking the door to
Reagan's room. It was pitch black. All I could hear was the quiet
snores of a sleeping man. As he breathed, the covered mound
moved up and down in a peaceful rhythm.

"Governor?" I said, too loudly.

A grunt, and a repositioning of the pillow, then, "Huh?"

"It's eight o'clock," I protested.

"Yeah?"

"Well, you're going to be inaugurated in a few hours as the fortieth president," I advised.

"Do I have to?"

If I had ever doubted Reagan's ability to handle pressure, I could have doubted it no longer. Here was a man very confident of his ability to cope with whatever lay ahead.

I accompanied the Reagans to the White House Blue Room where the customary coffee was to take place with the incoming and outgoing residents. I sat with the extended Reagan family and his closest advisers, many of whom, like me, were from California. Few, if any, of the Carter inner circle were there....

After a brief but somewhat disconcerting delay, President Carter arrived. He was a wreck—pale, even ashen. He must have been working the phones all night, still trying to slay the dragon that haunted his presidency [the American hostages in Tehran]. The mood in the Blue Room was cordial, but just barely. Carter was so determined to finish the job at hand he barely said anything to Reagan....

When we got to the Capitol, Reagan pulled me aside. Instead of feeling slighted, he was deeply moved by Carter's determination to see our people free. Reagan himself was becoming increasingly agitated that a handful of Iranian zealots could bring a sitting American president to his knees. He genuinely felt for Carter and understood entirely what was going through his mind.

Later, in the holding room, Reagan waved me over.

"What is it, Governor?" I said, calling him by that title for the last time in my life.

Based on the intelligence information he was provided, Reagan thought the release of the hostages was imminent. "If it happens, even during my Inaugural Address, I want you to tell me. Slip me a note. Interrupt me. Because if it happens, I want to bring Carter up to the platform. No country should embarrass and humiliate any president of the United States."

The opportunity never came. Twenty minutes after Reagan took the oath of office, word came to us that the hostages were in fact free. At the time, the new president was having a traditional lunch with the Senate leadership. I wrote out a quick note and made my way toward President Reagan. Without looking at the note, he instinctively knew what happened. He read it and let out a long, silent breath and smiled. America had a clean slate—and a new president. He knew that the Iranians did this to embarrass Carter. You would never hear Reagan boast that he had anything to do with the release of the hostages.

AN EERIE SILENCE

THE DAY WOULD COME WHEN I WOULD SEE Ronald Wilson Reagan for the last time in my life. His Alzheimer's had ratcheted up its already tight grip on the president's mind. Nancy had let it be known that she was soon going to restrict visitors to immediate family, so I needed to schedule my final good-bye.

In a way, I was almost relieved it would be my last time seeing Reagan. Unlike Nancy, I don't think I'm strong enough to bear such close witness to the man's decline.

By ending visits, Nancy was clearly acting in her husband's best interests, but I think in the back of her mind she was also protecting his friends. They shouldn't have to see him at his worst. She would not let the good times be elbowed out of the way by the invisible thief of memories....

As I pushed the door open, the knob for some reason slipped out of my hand, and the door thumped loudly against the stop. Ronald Reagan was sitting at his desk, reading a large book. Despite the noise, he didn't look up.

My eyes traveled around the office, noting changes. I wondered if Nancy had slowly begun removing things as the disease made its progress. There were far fewer paintings on the wall. Small stacks of books lined the room on the floor. It looked like he was preparing for a move. Certainly, this was no longer the Oval Office West.

I refocused my gaze on Reagan. He looked pretty good, I thought. Blue suit, French cuffs—for a man then in his late eighties, he was well turned-out. Some things never change, thank God. Finally, though, I realized that I could stand there all day and he wouldn't notice me. I'd have to take charge if there was going to be any conversation.

"Hi," I blurted out too loudly as I moved awkwardly toward his desk. I began shifting the leather datebook I habitually carry to my left hand, preparing to grasp once again the firm hand of my old friend and boss.

Only his head moved as he finally looked up. His gaze, so questioning and unrecognizing, was new to me. "Yes," he said. His voice was polite, as always, but he spoke with a tone I had never heard from him before. His hands stayed on his book.

With that, he resumed his reading and said nothing more. I stood there confused and saddened. He had no idea who I was, but I wasn't giving up yet. Quietly placing my datebook on the corner of his otherwise barren desk, I sat in a chair to his left and then pulled it closer to him, determined to get his attention.

"Whatcha reading?" I asked jovially.

For years, as Reagan and I crisscrossed the continent together, reading had been part of our routine. I'd settle into my seat on the plane and crack open some *New York Times* bestselling novel. After getting his sack of peanuts and icy Coca-Cola, Reagan would begin thumbing through the reams of memos and briefing documents that made up his "must read" file. Then, almost always, he'd set his papers briefly aside and, with a hint of envy and curiosity, ask me about my book.

Now, that time suddenly seemed so long ago. There was a pained look on Reagan's face as he answered my question. "A book" was all he said, and he looked back down.

I sat still for maybe three minutes as it dawned on me that I'd gone about this visit all wrong. I'd bulldozed in on him, trying to act like the old friend I was, but he saw only an intruder. I stood and moved slowly next to him, and as I did so, he looked up and gave me a half smile. Grateful for even a modicum of his confidence, I walked behind him and watched his busy fingers move from left to right on the large yellowing pages.

"What book?" I asked, finally focusing on it.

"A horse book," he said quietly.

For the first time, I looked at what he was holding in his hands and realized it was a picture book about Traveller, General Robert E. Lee's horse. I felt like crying.

I'd been told that when his staff cleaned out Reagan's old desk in his Century City office … they came upon a well-thumbed, time-worn letter from his mother in the top drawer. The content was nothing special—Nelle had sent it when he first moved to California decades ago—but clearly he had kept it close at hand as a reminder of a mother's love. Watching him now, as his finger worked laboriously across the page, I remembered the advice Nelle had given him years and years ago: "If you learn to love reading, you will never be alone."

Today, I was the lonely one. I must have said something as I turned and left the office—"It's wonderful seeing you," maybe. "I've got to go now." But I no longer remember what it was, and the man I had come to see wouldn't have heard it in any event. Ronald Reagan had heeded his mother and lost himself in a peaceful, solitary place.

Man of the Year 1981

OUT OF THE PAST, FRESH CHOICES FOR THE FUTURE

REPRINTED FROM THE JAN. 5, 1981, ISSUE OF TIME

BY ROGER ROSENBLATT AND
LAURENCE I. BARRETT

Roger Rosenblatt was an associate editor of TIME
and Laurence I. Barrett a senior correspondent.

O N AN AFTERNOON IN EARLY DECEMBER, LOS
Angeles was in the 60s and Ronald Reagan looked
like a dream. He was wearing a blue-and-green
wool tartan jacket, a purple tie, white shirt, white
handkerchief, black pants and black loafers with
gold along the tops. Who else could dress that way? He settled
back on a couch in a living room so splurged with color that even
the black seemed exuberant. A florist must have decorated it.
A florist must have decorated his voice. He was talking about
job hunting as a kid in his home town of Dixon, Ill., telling an
American success story he has told a hundred times before. He
seemed genuinely happy to hear it again. No noise made its way
up to the house on Pacific Palisades, except for the occasional
yip of a dog, and, of course, the eternal sound of California—the
whir of a well-tuned car. Outside, the Secret Service patrolled the
bougainvillea on streets with liquid, Spanish names. Reagan's
face was ruddy, in bloom, growing younger by the second.

At week's end he would be expected at the convocation of conservatives for the *National Review*'s 25th anniversary dinner in
the Plaza Hotel in New York City. Reagan would not show—a
mix-up in his calendar. Riled, his hosts would sing his praises
over dessert nonetheless. He was the answer to their prayers,
after all; the essential reason for the elegant, confident glow of
the evening. Editor William F. Buckley Jr. would shine quietly,
modestly. Others, like Publisher William Rusher, would exhort
the assembled "to stamp out any remaining embers of liberal-
ism." A war whoop was in the air—black tie, to be sure—but still
the unmistakable sound of a faction reprieved, at last in power,
thanks to the boyish man at the other end of the country, whose
time had definitely come.

As for the cause of the celebration, his rise seems astonish-
ing. It began in October 1964 when, as co-chairman of California Citizens for Goldwater, he gave his "A Time for Choosing"

television speech, a speech so tough that Goldwater himself was skittish about letting it air. Reagan ended the talk with "You and I have a rendezvous with destiny," and was at least half right. So mesmerizing was his performance, so quick in its effect, that California businessmen swamped him like groupies, formed a "Friends of Ronald Reagan" committee, begged him to run for Governor. He had to be pushed. Yet in 1966 the former star of *Juke Girl* snatched the governorship of California by a million votes from incumbent Edmund G. ("Pat") Brown, who must have thought he was the victim of an accident. (Reagan also starred in *Accidents Will Happen*.)

In fact, there has been a remarkably accidental air about Reagan's career; it has always borne the quality of something he could take or leave. The image of the non-politician running for office, antilogical as it is, has had its practical advantages, but it is also authentic. Because Reagan knows who he is, he knows what he wants. After a halfhearted run at Nixon for the Republican presidential nomination in 1968, he returned to California for a second term as Governor. But in 1976, after an all-out and failed attempt to capture his party's nomination, he genuinely did not wish to be Gerald Ford's Vice President. When Ford's invitation went to Bob Dole, Reagan loyalists were crestfallen, reading in that rebuff the end of their man's life in politics. Only Reagan took it well, content to settle forever on his ranch, if it came to that, but also believing (as few others did) that even at age 65 you can run into luck.

Four years later, his party, now confirmed in its conservatism, turned to him like a heliotrope. He was lucky to run against (Eastern, brittle) George Bush for the nomination; he was lucky to be beaten early in Iowa, before the so-called momentum against him was real; he was lucky to have Jimmy Carter as his opponent. On the night of Nov. 4, 1980, just 16 years after he had spoken his mind in behalf of a man too far right to be elected President, the amateur politician who will become 70 in February watched state after state turn in his direction.

For that, in part, Reagan is TIME's Man of the Year—for having risen so smoothly and gracefully to the most powerful and visible position in the world. He is also the idea of the year, his triumph being philosophical as well as personal. He has revived the Republican Party, and has garnered high initial hopes, even from many who opposed him, both because of his personal style and because the U.S. is famished for cheer. On Jan. 20 Reagan and the idea he embodies will both emerge from their respective seclusions with a real opportunity to change the direction and tone of the nation.

Reagan is also TIME's Man of the Year because he stands at the end of 1980 looking ahead, while the year behind him smolders in pyres. The events of any isolated year can be made to seem exceptionally grim, but one has to peer hard to find elevating moments in 1980. Only Lech Walesa's stark heroism in Poland sent anything resembling a thrill into the world. The national strike he led showed up Communism as a failure—a thing not done in the Warsaw Pact countries. Leonid Brezhnev, a different sort of strongman, had to send troops to Poland's borders, in case that country, like Czechoslovakia and Hungary before it, should prove in need of "liberation."

Otherwise, the year was consumed with the old war-and-death business. Afghanistan enters the year as a prisoner of its "liberating" neighbor; Iran and Iraq close the year at each other's throats. In between, Cambodians are starved out of existence; terrorists go about murdering 80 or more in Bologna, and a mere four outside a Paris synagogue. In Turkey, political violence kills 2,000; in El Salvador, more than 9,000 die in that country's torment. All this on top of natural disasters: Mount St. Helens erupts in Washington State; one earthquake in Algeria kills 3,000; another in Italy takes the same toll. Human enterprise is tested, and responds with black market coffins.

In February Americans flinch at an inflation rate of 18% that drops to a hardly bearable 12.7% as the year ends. February is also the month when the U.S. hockey team's victory over the Soviets ignites national pride. But in April the U.S. boycotts the Summer Olympic Games to protest the Soviet invasion of Afghanistan. In May Cuban refugees flee Castro, and the U.S. greets them at first with an "open arms" policy, then a state of emergency in Florida, then a closing of the open arms—the entire pilgrimage eventually capped off with riots at Eglin Air Force Base and later at Fort Chaffee. Vernon Jordan is shot in May as well. In June science announces a breakthrough in recombinant DNA research, raising high hopes of cancer cures along with specters of genetic

> He is also the idea of the year,
> his triumph being philosophical
> as well as personal.

engineering and Andromeda strains. The prime lending rate at major banks soars to 21.5% in December, all but ensuring that 1981 will begin with a recession.

Old orders pass: Prime Minister Ohira in Japan; the Shah in Egypt; and Tito, who one thought would live forever. In the background, like presiding ghosts, the hostages in Iran serve as emblems of national impotence; Walter Cronkite's counting of the days growing weary and meaningless among Milquetoast threats and a tragic rescue fiasco. As if to sustain the world's heartache, the year heads toward Christmas with the killing of a Beatle.

In 1953 Robert Lowell said the "Republic summons Ike" because "the mausoleum [was] in her heart." In 1980 the Republic summoned Ronald Reagan. Why?

History rarely moves openly toward its main players. Usually a central figure is perceived as evolving only in retrospect, and that could well happen four years from now, when the country may acknowledge that Ronald Reagan was the only man who could possibly have pulled the U.S. out of its doldrums. For now, in prospect, that certainly cannot be said. Reagan is an experiment, a chance. For all the happy feelings his good nature generates, the cool fact of American life is that most of the country is still from Missouri, and much is yet to be proved.

In this light it may be useful to remember first that Reagan's ten-point popular victory was not assured until the final days of the campaign. As deeply soured on the Carter Administration as most of the electorate was, it also withheld its approval of the competition until the last minute. Quietly, privately and perhaps a little grimly, most Americans had probably decided that Carter had had it as early as 18 months before November. Their main reason was the economy, but there was Carter himself, a man who also started out riding the country's high hopes (a TIME Man of the Year in 1976), and who was perhaps most bitterly resented for shrinking those hopes down to the size of a presidency characterized by small people, small talk and small matters. He made Americans feel two things they are not used to feeling, and will not abide. He made them feel puny and he made them feel insecure.

That Reagan beat such a man is a feat of circumstances as much as of personal strength. Right-wingers like to crow that the country veered sharply to the right when it turned to Reagan, but the probable truth of the matter is that most of the country had simply stepped firmly to the right of center. As conservatives sensed, the country had been an incubative conservative since the late '60s. Only Nixon's muck-up could have delayed their eventual birth and triumph. Sick and tired of the vast, clogged federal machine; sick and tired of being broke; fed up with useless programs, crime, waste, guilt; not to mention shame in the eyes of the world—derision from our enemies, dismay from our allies—fed up with all that, and to put a fine point on it, fed up with Jimmy Carter, what else would the nation do but hang a right?

The fascinating thing is how determined a swing it was. Reagan's pollster Richard Wirthlin found that voters, even at the end of the campaign, believed that Reagan was more likely to start an unnecessary war than Carter, and that Carter was much more sensitive to the poor and the elderly. Still, the right prevailed. The New Deal was out of steam; in the long run it ensured its own obsolescence by giving the workingman the wherewithal to turn Republican. Even so, his paycheck was inadequate. Everything seemed inadequate. The country had to move on, but it was not moving anywhere. Enter Reagan (with jubilation and a mandate).

That mandate is specific: to control inflation, to reduce unnecessary governmental interference in private lives and in business, to reassert America's prominence in the world. That is all there is to it, and that is plenty. The mandate does not necessarily include far-right hit lists, censorship, the absence of gun control, prayer in schools and a constitutional amendment banning abortion. These things are significant if problematical, but they do not represent majority wishes. Nor does the Reagan mandate suggest approval of a national pulpit for Jerry Falwell's lethal sweet talk or of the National Conservative Political Action Committee (NCPAC), whose liberal-hunting leaders have been jumping up and down like Froggie the Gremlin since Nov. 4. The majority voted for Reagan because he appeared to be a reasonable man, and a reasonable presidency is what the country expects.

Still, it is not only the anticipation of Reagan's reasonableness that has hopes high at the moment. Pennsylvania's Republican Governor Richard Thornburgh explains the Reagan election in terms of ideas: "The status of the individual in society, fiscal integrity, the idea of true federalism, the idea of Government closer to the people, the idea of the toughness of the American fiber, which means a firm line with criminals at home and with our adversaries abroad. With Reagan's election, Republican principles hold the high ground, the principles which put together the real genesis of the Reagan victory. Those principles are now a majority view."

That is true enough, but Republicanism is also changing. During all the years the Democrats were in power, their party developed a kind of character, one that reached a pinnacle of form in John Kennedy—that is, the character of the interesting party, the party of real intellectual movement, the party of the mind. Conversely, the G.O.P. was the party of the pocketbook, the pinstripe and the snort. Goodbye to all that. The G.O.P. is now by far the more interesting of the two parties. And much of the anticipation of the Reagan presidency has to do with the fact that people recognize that an idea is taking shape.

The man at the center of this idea appears smaller than he is. At 6 ft. 1 in., 185 lbs., his body is tight, as tight as it can be on a large frame, though there is no sign of pulling or strain. It is the body of an actor, of someone used to being scrutinized from all angles, so it has all but willed as tidy and organized an appearance as possible. His size also seems an emblem of his modesty. Lyndon Johnson used to enter a room and rape it. Reagan seems to be in a continual state of receding, a posture that makes strangers lean toward him. In a contest for the same audience, he would draw better than Johnson.

The voice goes perfectly with the body. No President since Kennedy has had a voice at once so distinctive and beguiling. It too recedes at the right moments, turning mellow at points of intensity. When it wishes to be most persuasive, it hovers barely above a whisper so as to win you over by intimacy, if not by substance. This is style, but not sham. Reagan believes everything he says, no matter how often he has said it, or if he has said it in the same words every time. He likes his voice, treats it like a guest. He makes you part of the hospitality.

It was that voice that carried him out of Dixon and away from the Depression, the voice that more than any single attribute got him where he is. On that smoky blue December afternoon in Pacific Palisades he was telling the old story again—about his job hunting in 1932, about heading for Chicago, where "a very kind woman" at NBC told him to start out in the sticks. So he drove around to radio station WOC in Davenport, Iowa, where he made his pitch to the program director, Peter MacArthur, an arthritic old Scotsman who hobbled on two canes. Reagan, of course, had that voice, and he had played football for Eureka College. But MacArthur said that he had just hired someone else, and Reagan stomped off muttering, "How the hell do you get to be a sports announcer if you can't get into a station?" The delivery is perfect—plaintive,

> Reagan seems to be in a continual state of receding, a posture that makes strangers lean toward him.

sore. Something wonderful is bound to happen.

"I walked down the hall to the operator, and fortunately the elevator wasn't at that floor. And while I was waiting, I heard this thumping down the hall and this Scotch burr very profanely saying (in a Reagan Scotch burr), 'Wait up, ya big so and so.'" And what did MacArthur say? Something about sports, of course. And what did MacArthur ask? "Do you think you could tell me about a football game and make me see it?" And could Ronald Reagan do that then and there? On the folk tale goes, fresh as a daisy, full of old hope and heartbeats.

In the pinch, Reagan fell back on describing a game he had played in for Eureka. "So when the light went on I said, 'Here we are going into the fourth quarter on a cold November afternoon, the long blue shadows settling over the field, the wind whipping in through the end of the stadium'—hell, we didn't have a stadium at Eureka, we had grandstands—and I took it up to the point in which there were 20 seconds to go and we scored the winning touchdown. As a blocking guard, I was supposed to get the first man in the secondary to spring our back loose, and I didn't get him. I missed him. And I've never known to this day how Bud Cole got by and scored that touchdown. But in the rebroadcast I nailed the guy on defense. I took him down with a magnificent block."

Cheers and laughter. Who would not hire this man? Humility, a sense of proportion, gentle humor. Bless the elevator operator; bless the crippled Scotsman. Who would doubt that even now, from time to time, the Governor dreams of the fancy footwork of the ever elusive Bud Cole?

Of course, the anecdote gives everything and nothing. In the movies, *The Story of Ronald Reagan* might be built of such stuff, like the "story" of Jim Thorpe, but not a life; the life has to be discovered elsewhere. At least the facts pile up neatly: born Feb. 6, 1911, Tampico, Ill.; son of John Edward and Nelle Wilson Reagan; younger brother of Neil Reagan, now a retired advertising executive in California. After Tampico the Reagans move around for a while and then to Dixon, a back-porch and lemonade town on the Rock River. Father is a sometime shoe salesman and a sometime alcoholic. Mother, a Scottish Protestant; father, Irish Catholic. Ronald takes the faith of his mother.

At high school in Dixon, "Dutch" plays football. His eyes are weak; he is undersized for his age; still he plays the line. He also joins the basketball team, takes part in track meets, is elected president of the student body. Along the way, he works as a lifeguard at a local river and rescues 77 people, a record of sorts, preserved in notches on a log. He is Midwest perfect, down to the requisite transgression. Mellow on homemade wine one night, he mounts a traffic stand and bellows "Twinkle, twinkle, little star." On to

Eureka, where he wins letters in football, track and swimming, and joins the dramatics club. (Here the repeated good lines: "Nature was trying to tell me something. Namely, my heart is a ham loaf.") He pays his way through school, his family so poor they move into a single-bedroom apartment with an electric plate. Neighbors carry supper over to them on trays. At Eureka, he is again elected student-body president. In a regional drama competition, his performance as a shepherd wins honors. The idea of working in radio occurs to him as a halfway measure between acting and respectability. He lights out for Chicago, and the rest is folklore.

The element missing in such accounts is what it feels like to be Ronald Reagan. His autobiography, *Where's the Rest of Me?* takes its title from the most memorable line he ever delivered as an actor, when his legs were amputated in *Kings Row*. As his presidency goes on, that title is bound to turn on him, as *Why Not the Best?* turned on Jimmy Carter, though with Reagan the question will be less accusative than mystifying. That self-diminution, the trustworthiness, the aura of the towhead, the voice—all comprise a figure one takes to the heart. But where is he in this process? What clobbers him? He offers no signs now. Back in Dixon he did offer something, however small.

He wrote a poem in high school and called it "Life," as all high school poems must be called. It went as follows:

I wonder what it's all about, and why
We suffer so, when little things go wrong?
We make our life a struggle,
When life should be a song.

Our troubles break and drench us.
Like spray on the cleaving prow
Of some trim Gloucester schooner.
As it dips in a graceful bow....

But why does sorrow drench us
When our fellow passes on?
He's just exchanged life's dreary dirge
For an eternal life of song....

Millions have gone before us,
And millions will come behind,
So why do we curse and fight
At a fate both wise and kind?

We hang onto a jaded life
A life full of sorrow and pain.
A life that warps and breaks us,
And we try to run through it again.

The poem is odd, baleful—not an unusual tone for a teenager generally, but neither is it what we would expect of the peppy, clean-cut teen-ager that was young Dutch Reagan. Examined under a sad light, "Life" is the poem of a boy who either wants to drown or is at least considering the possibility. The first stanza is cheery enough, but it really belongs to another poem. The sense of advocated surrender in the final stanza is unmistakable. Not that Reagan would be unusual in having contemplated death as a way out of adolescence, but one does not think of his early life as having been touched with "sorrow and pain." Of course, the poem might simply have been the product of a bad moment. But even a momentary touch of desperation is interesting in such a man.

Usually, Reagan's assessments of his childhood are entirely wistful, but there was a hint of something else when he was asked recently if he ever saw his father in himself as a parent. His answer: "Yes, and maybe sometimes too much so. I don't know how to describe it because neither of my parents ever had anything in the line of a formal education, and yet there was a freedom to make decisions, and sometimes I find that maybe I go too far in that." That freedom to make decisions fits well with Reagan's political philosophy, but his answer leaves out a negative element of his own performance as a parent. A parent's philosophy of freedom leaves the parent free as well.

The main characteristics that Reagan displays —good humor, modesty, patience—are the attributes of fatherhood at its best. And from all appearances Reagan would seem to have been the compassionate father, the father to turn to in times of grief and disarray; the father of rich stories and silly jokes. Instead, his relationship with all four children—Maureen and Mike, his children with Jane Wyman, and Patti and Ron, his children with Nancy—seems to be that of deliberately created distances. The physical distances, the fact that the children were shipped off to boarding schools at young ages, seem an adjunct of the emotional distances—though the first two children lived with Wyman after she divorced him, so in their case some of the distancing was circumstantial. As for Patti and Ron, Reagan admits that he did not spend much time with them but blames his life as a celebrity and not his own desires. He tells dolefully of taking Patti to the opening of Disneyland and being beset by autograph hounds, spoiling a normal, happy family excursion.

Given that other celebrities manage to spend time with their children, Reagan's explanation does not make much sense. Still, there is no doubt that it makes sense to him. The regret he expresses about not having been more attentive to the children is sincere, if low level. Now, the children grown, they all seem much closer than before, which is interesting, as it suggests that Reagan, who bears much of the aspect of an adorable child himself, simply gets along better with grownups. The unceremonious wedding of young Ron a few weeks after the election offers a public sign that some vestiges of the old distances remain.

Yet in the odd child-parent pattern of the Reagan family, Ron's decision to marry suddenly with barely a last-minute word to his folks is perfectly traditional. It is widely known that Ron's parents have not managed to see a single ballet performance of their son, who is clearly very good, having been selected to the Joffrey second company, and is their son nonetheless. Ron talks of his parents with much affection. But these absences are strange and go back a ways. Son Mike was a successful motorboat racer; Reagan did not see a single race. Mike, a star quarterback at Judson School in Scottsdale, Ariz., was named Player of the Year in 1964. Reagan saw not a game.

The family tradition that he was upholding by such omissions is that his own father rarely managed to see him and Brother Neil play football. Neil Reagan notes the fact today, conceding that his father's lack of interest was odd, but consistent with the ideal of "independence" among the Reagans. Yet it takes an act of will not to watch one's children in a moment important to their self esteem. One almost has to actively deny the desire to show pride and affection; no child could mistake the effort—unless, of course, the pride and affection were purely superficial. The great puzzlement about Ronald Reagan, in fact, is exactly how much of him lies hidden. He has lived a charmed life on the surface—many people do—but it is disconcerting, to say the least, to unravel Reagan like H.G. Wells' invisible man, only to discover that when you get the bandages off, the center is not to be seen.

Still, after listening to Reagan, it would be impossible to conclude that he did not love his children. It would be easier to conclude that he did not know how to love his children, when they were children, just as it is possible to assume that his father did not know how to love him. There is an abiding compassion in Reagan for his father, for his father's drinking —the "sickness," as his mother explained it. The story is now famous of his finding his father passed out on the front porch and bearing him inside. Nor is there any sign that Reagan's father was anything but a man of high natural instincts, like the son who inherited his looks, capable of fierce rage at racial or religious bigotry. But neither are there signs of real father-to-son love. And the fact that Reagan's father was an alcoholic, albeit "periodic," as Reagan is quick to explain, must have alloyed young Ronald's feelings for his father as much with dread as with sympathy.

One thing the children of alcoholics often have in common is an uncommon sense of control—control of themselves and control of their world, which they know from harsh experience can turn perilous at the click of a door latch. Not that Jack Reagan was known to be a mean drunk; but brutal or not, all alcoholics create states of alarm in their children. They learn a kind of easygoing

> It would be impossible to conclude that he did not love his children. It would be easier to conclude that he did not know how to love his children.

formality early on, like the Secret Service, and they are often acutely alert to danger, for the very reason that the parent's binges are periodic. That receding look and sound of Reagan may be the hallmarks of such control. One cannot retain anger in the presence of such a man, and thus in a sense he makes fathers of us all.

In fact, Reagan seems ever to place himself in the position of being adopted. He has, in a sense, been adopted by a plethora of fathers over the years, wealthy patrons and protectors who recognized a hope for the country's future in their favorite son. Yet Reagan is also a genuine loner. His ranch is a true retreat for him, a state of mind, and perhaps an emblem of his achievement, of the independence he was taught to prize. Solitude and self-reliance, the two essential American virtues that Emerson named, are found in him naturally. On the ranch he can be free—not "on" to audiences. The only odd thing in the picture is that such a loner would choose to give his life to lines of work that demand continuous performance.

The combination of showmanship and privacy is unusual, but the combination of that sense of control with genuine good nature is extraordinary. Conventionally, a severe sense of control is used to harness rage or malice; Reagan seems incapable of either. The effect of that combination, however, is not entirely sanguine. Twenty-five years ago, Neil dreamed up an elaborate and touching Christmas present for his kid brother. He found an impoverished family with a father who was a drunk and out of work, and Neil took the wife and child on a shopping spree. The parallels to the Reagans' own childhood are evident, and whatever moved Neil to emphasize the parallels remains obscure. But the gift was one of immense ingenuity and generosity—because the shopping spree was given in Ronald's name. Yet when it was presented to Reagan, along with a poem Neil wrote for the occasion, Ronald reacted by saying, "Gee, that's keen." It is difficult to know if he was moved or not, but he certainly did not wish to give the impression (satisfaction) of having been moved.

When Campaign Manager John Sears was determined to get Mike Deaver, one of the closest friends of both the Reagans, out of the 1980 organization, Reagan let it happen. He said he did not like it, but he went along anyway, choosing pragmatism over loyalty. There are other examples of cool calculation that seem out of place in what is patently a good heart. The feeling one takes from a conversation with Reagan—and it is very quiet and faint—is that his geniality is equal to his fears. What, specifically, he is afraid of is a secret, as it is with most successful people. But there is no secret about his ability to do a kind of stylistic judo on a potential threat. The voice softens to music; the eyes grow helpless, worried.

TIME: "You were quoted as having said that you had read Norman Podhoretz's *The Present Danger* and thought it was a very important book. Is that accurate? Did you admire that book when it came out?"

REAGAN: "I read it. [Backs off at once; eyes are shy with surprise; sounds as if he's being accused of something, or as if he is about to be tested.] I don't recall ever having anything to say about it. [Hesitates, but seeing no traps, relaxes slightly.] But I did read it [some firmness now] and do believe that it makes a great deal of sense [confidence restored]."

None of this is to suggest that Reagan resembles a haunted or threatened man. In a lifetime one does not encounter half a dozen people so authentically at ease with themselves. Reagan is a natural; he knows it. His intuitions are always in tune, and he trusts his own feelings. All his political opinions have been born of feelings—the passionate antagonism toward Big Government resulting from his boyhood observations of Dixon and his own experiences with the progressive income tax once he returned from the military; his staunch anti-Communism from his days with the Screen Actors Guild in the late 1940s, when he packed a pistol for self-protection. He will read up on a subject once it has initially been proved on his pulses, but he does not take his main ideas from printed words. In that process of intellection he is classically American—the natural man whose intelligence lies not in book learning but in right instincts. Reagan regularly reads conservative journals of opinion and his share of newspapers and magazines and contemporary books about politics, but no author seems to have been especially influential in his life. Yet he is able, by employing a kind of trick of memory, to dredge up whole passages of things he read as far back as 40 years ago. Like many politicians, he probably uses reading the way one might use friends. Instead of his going to books, they come to him.

This sense of his integrity, of his thoroughgoing self-knowledge is a major asset. When he was making *Dark Victory* (yes, he was there, well behind Bette Davis, George Brent and Humphrey Bogart), the director (Edmund Goulding) bawled him out for playing a scene too simply and sincerely. "He didn't get what he wanted, whatever the hell that was," Reagan recalls, "and I ended up not delivering the line the way my instinct told me it should be delivered. It was bad."

Now, considerably freer to follow his instincts, his lines are delivered with consistent effect—simply and sincerely. At the close of the Carter television debate he posed several semi-rhetorical questions that are now said to have sealed his victory: "Are you better off than you were four years ago? Is it easier for you to go and buy things in the stores?" And so forth. There is first the brilliance of the baby talk—"to go and buy things in the stores." But the real power in those questions came from the delivery, which if managed by a less sensitive speaker could have produced something strident, or assured, or worse, argumentative. Instead, Reagan's pitch trembled between helplessness and fellow feeling; it was to himself that he was talking; he who could not go and buy things in the stores. The U.S. was in a sad mess, not an infuriating one. Only a calm though suffering voice could rescue it.

Where more hard-nosed politicians will talk ceaselessly about polling techniques or some son of a bitch in a rebellious precinct, Reagan will talk about the art of public speaking. Even though he is a virtuoso, he works at that art, primarily because he is a politician only of the essentials, and knows, as his admired Franklin Roosevelt knew, that to reach and please the public is to put first things first. One sign of his amazing success as a speaker is that his plentiful gaffes are not only forgiven; even better, they are forgotten. Speaking in Columbus last summer, he deliberately made an error, substituting the word depression for recession in order to reinforce a point. The alteration set off a small squall of technical retractions by one of his economics advisers, Alan Greenspan, but the point was reinforced. His sense of timing is almost always a thing of beauty. After the "depression" error, instead of dropping the matter, he traded on it: "If he [Carter] wants a definition, I'll give him one. [Audience is on the alert for something punchy, perhaps funny.] Recession [split-second pause] is when your neighbor loses his job. Depression [same pause; audience grows eager] is when you lose yours. [Chuckles and titters; audience wonders if there will be a third part to the definition.] And recovery [audience gears itself for a laugh] is when Jimmy Carter loses his [kaboom]."

The opposition's book on Reagan (by now a public document) is that he is always underestimated. That too is a mark of the natural man—the fox taken for a fool who winds up taking the

> One sign of his amazing success as a speaker is that his plentiful gaffes are not only forgiven; even better, they are forgotten.

taker. Yet there is no Volpone slyness in Reagan. If he has been underestimated, it may be that he gives every sign of underestimating himself—not as a tactic, but honestly. So wholly without self-puffery is he that he places the burden of judging him entirely on others, and since he is wholly without self-puffery, the judgment is almost always favorable. He simply appeals to people, and despite his years, there is hardly anyone of any age who would not feel protective of him, would not wish him to succeed, would not forget the mistakes, who would not corral him in the hall and give him a job. Again this is not a tactic. It may well be his soul.

Does this mean, then, that his soul is not his own? The question is urgent in the minds of those who fear that the Reagan presidency will be shaped and conducted by the God-toting religicos or the fever-swamp conservatives who exult in the hopes that they are free at last. The answer to that question is no, but it ought not necessarily put the worriers at ease. Reagan's soul is his own, yet what sort of soul is it? For those who have observed Reagan lo these many years, the answer is clearly and consistently a most conservative soul, notwithstanding the formulaic chitchat about his having once been a hemophiliac liberal, which is simply a device for implying that policies aside, his heart is still with the people. A more precise question is: What sort of mind has Reagan? How intelligent is he? But with "natural" men, intelligence is not so readily definable.

For the moment, what we can see in Reagan is a vision of America, of America's future, at once so simple and deep as to incur every emotion from elation to terror. It is a little like the vision of the Hudson River school of painting—the brooding serenity of turquoise skies, patriarchal clouds and trees, very still, doll-like people (white and red), infinite promise, potential self-deception and, above all, perfect containment—the individual and the land, man and God locked in a snakeless Eden. James Fenimore Cooper wrote a novel, *Satanstoe*, about such a place, an ideal America in which everyone ruled his own vast estate, his own civilization. Whether or not Reagan sees Rancho del Cielo or Pacific Palisades as Satanstoe, his dream of the New World is as old as Cooper's.

At the center of that dream is the word freedom; it is a key word with Reagan, and it is the word at the center of all American dreams, from the beautiful to the murderous. Reagan's version seems to center largely on the question of free enterprise: "[Americans] have always known that excessive bureaucracy is the enemy of excellence and compassion." True. Therefore, freedom must be the ally of excellence and compassion. Sometimes. Since Reagan's way of understanding things is personal, he puts it thus: He dug a pond on his own property, and now if he wants to stock that pond with fish, he has to get a fishing license to catch his own fish. Bingo. If the vision of boundless freedom were to consist solely of being able to fish one's own ponds, who would have trouble siding with Reagan's idea?

But there is no particular trick in making a buffoon of federal regulations. Things grow more problematical when one tries to extend such reasonable complaints to a general political philosophy, and talk—as Reagan does talk—of putting "the Federal Government back in the business of doing the things the Constitution says are its prime functions: to keep internal order, to protect us in our national security from outside aggression and to provide a stable currency for our commerce and trade." Very well. But such a definition omits the "general welfare" clause. And in practical terms, Reagan undoubtedly does not intend to dismantle the N.L.R.B., Social Security, unemployment insurance and other such encroachments on pure freedom that are here to stay. So, what does he mean?

However vague and simplified Reagan's idea of freedom may be, it touches a central chord in American thought, a chord that will sound when people start to fear that the future is over, as they did during the Carter Administration. The fact that Reagan speaks for the virtues of both the past and the future is reassuring, if safe, but the fact that his definition of freedom is essentially Western is more to the point. When Reagan speaks of freedom, he is speaking of freedom west of the Rockies. That is where he found his own best America; that is where he continues to find his personal and philosophical solace; that is what he wishes for the country at large—a California dream, an endless prospect of gold and greenery and don't fence me in.

That California has come to embody such a vision of boundlessness is a little strange, since the dream of California is as much the dream of disappointment as of hope—the dream of arriving at virgin territory, of messing it up, and having gone as far as one can go, of having nowhere to turn but back. As Kevin Starr pointed out in his *Americans and the California Dream*, California has always stood for something mystical in American life; it has not suffered the tragic historical burdens of the East and South, and it has seemed determined to make itself as much a folk tale as a habitat. But just as it has always insisted on its eternal newness and promise, it has also represented the dead end of the New World, the end of exploration, recalling all the mistakes of every past civilization. One reason that Balboa (Keats mistakenly wrote Cortes) might have stood "silent upon a peak in Darien" is that he realized there was no place else on earth to travel to. Or as a Walt Whitman character said in "Facing West from California's Shores": "Where is what I started for so long ago? And why is it yet unfound?"

Reagan does not ask that question, nor does he stand silent upon a peak in Pacific Palisades and brood about paradise lost. His California dream remains unsullied. America is still the land of perpetual opportunity, and every man gloriously for himself. Economics fits into this vision neatly, since California happened to provide a fine justification for capitalism by producing gold from the earth like a health food. If there were a California Ocean school of painting, it would consist of avocados in the foreground and a range of office buildings behind. Perhaps that is Reagan's interior skyline.

Theoretically such a vision should produce the government that Reagan has promised, the kind that governs least. If corporate America is part of nature—of the nature of the country, the nature of man—then it must be free to grow to its fullest capacity, like an individual. Tax cuts, reduced federal interference and other prods to Big Business (including the corporate character of the Cabinet appointments) are simply ways of making pioneers of businessmen, of restoring some of the old make-a-buck fire. Yet the character of the Reagan Administration will not depend wholly on his political vision, which in any case will be modified by wary liberal Democrats in Congress, by the normal exigencies of the modern presidency and by his own ability to compromise. Rather the Reagan years are as likely to be shaped by the temperament and intelligence of the head man, and that is precisely why those years are so difficult to envisage.

If one were to take all of Reagan's qualities—the detachment, the self-knowledge, the great voice and good looks—and project them into the White House, he would have a first-class B-movie presidency. That is no insult. The best B movies, while not artistically exquisite, are often the ones that move us most because they move us directly, through straightforward characters, simple

> Intellectually, emotionally, Reagan lives in the past. That is where the broad vision comes from; the past is his future. But is it also the country's?

moral conflicts and idealized talk. Reagan once called himself "the Errol Flynn of B movies," which was astute (except that Errol Flynn was also the Errol Flynn of B movies). The President who remains above the fray yet is also capable of stirring the people is the kind of President of whose life B movies are made. After several years of *The Deer Hunter* and *All the President's Men*, perhaps *The Ronald Reagan Story* is just what the country ordered.

The trouble, however, since we are watching our lives and not a movie, is that in reality a detached presidency puts decisions in the hands of everyone else. No harm is done when the issues are trivial, but as the piecemeal nature of the Cabinet appointments has demonstrated, relying so totally on advisers is a dangerous game. The prospect grows considerably more troublesome when it comes to making major decisions. And there will be plenty of those as soon as Reagan takes office—all complicated and many urgent.

For starters, he faces an economic situation growing more frightening by the moment. Almost at once he will have to decide what to cut in this year's budget and where to attack the one for fiscal 1982, which is about to be submitted by Carter. These decisions will affect his proposed tax cuts and his plans to increase money for defense. They will also bear on whether or not he will have to cut real social welfare programs, not the "fat" he is accustomed to citing. On top of these, he faces rising unemployment, monstrous interest rates and U.S. industries (like cars) that are running on square wheels. And there are difficulties that are his, which he may not see. What happens to a black teen-ager in Harlem or Watts in a free enterprise system that leaves him free to go to hell?

In foreign affairs, everything in sight seems an emergency, from the hostages to the Polish frontier. Whatever happens in Poland, Reagan will not be overeager to negotiate an arms-control pact with the Soviets. What sort of agreement, then, will eventually be sought? Regarding the Third World, Reagan and his people have talked as if Soviet mischief making were the main problem, and also have come out strongly against organized terrorism, suggesting that the U.S. will send supplies to countries under siege by guerrillas. How does that position affect Latin America today, especially El Salvador skidding crazily toward a possible civil war? Given Third World realities, it is all very well to support anti-Communist regimes without too much worry about how democratic they are, but what if they are so discredited with their own people that they cannot survive? For cogent reasons, Reagan and his aides seem willing to downplay the human rights issue somewhat, but how will they deal with it in the context of Soviet Jews and other dissidents?

In the Middle East, how will he continue to placate both Israelis and Arabs? How will he reassure the allies of the U.S.'s renewed commitment? These are not the kinds of problems to be handled by subordinates, committees or forceless task forces. They require determination but also sophistication. They are to be handled by a President who studies, considers and knows what he wants.

In the broadest terms Reagan does know what he wants out of the next four years. But as those terms address specifics, that broad vision may prove inept. Intellectually, emotionally, Reagan lives in the past. That is where the broad vision comes from; the past is his future. But is it also the country's? Helen Lawton, a current resident of Dixon, Ill., and a loyal Reaganite, observed of her man: "Right now, in some ways, I think he'd love to go back to the good old days. In those days he didn't even realize he was poor because so many others were poor too. He wants the good life, not in terms of material things, but so that kids can have good times and strong family relationships. Yes, I think he would like to go back to how it used to be, but it's going to be difficult." That puts it mildly.

"All our great Presidents were leaders of thought at times when certain historic ideas in the life of the nation had to be clarified." So said Franklin Roosevelt, who was in a good position to know. The limits of freedom, our oldest idea, must be clarified now. Meanwhile the country is patently more hopeful about its future than it has been in a long while, much longer than the past four years; and to be fair to Jimmy Carter he was surely as much a casualty of the malaise he identified as he was its superintendent. When young man Reagan went West for the first time, the future clearly looked like the ranch or like Pacific Palisades, or perhaps both: the genteel and frontier traditions bound together by good manners and pluck. But when he turns eastward this month, the New World will be more complex, more shadowy and more terrifying for all its magnificent possibility.

An Interview with Ronald Reagan

The President-elect outlines his policies for home and abroad

BY LAURENCE I. BARRETT

As he looks ahead to his Administration, Ronald Reagan concedes that the worsening economy might delay his timetable for balancing the budget, but he still intends to cut taxes as well as spending. He wants to negotiate a new arms control pact with Moscow, but warns that an invasion of Poland could lead to a trade and diplomacy "quarantine" against the Soviet Union. [The threat, stemming from the Solidarity movement's promotion of workers' rights and social change, never materialized.] On other subjects, from welfare to the environment to human rights, he maintains his basic firm, conservative line.

Q. Sir, you have picked most of your Cabinet, conferred with President Carter, received scores of task force reports and explored the Washington Establishment. Have your views of the presidency and its challenges changed since the election?

A. No, I think I have always been well aware of the enormity of it, the difficulties, the fact that you cannot undo in a minute and a half what it has taken quite a long time to build up. I suppose if there is anything that has changed at all, it has been the deterioration of the economy, which makes the problem even more acute.

Q. Do you agree with a number of economists who are predicting that we are in for yet another downturn?

A. We have been on a downward slide for several weeks now. But that just strengthens my belief that this is the time for what we have been advocating, which is a totally different policy. And I would think that even if some people question that different policy or are not in complete agreement with my own faith in it, and others' faith in it, that at least they would recognize it is time for a change, time to try something different. I think that [the problems with the economy] will just mean that it will probably take a little longer for the effects to be seen.

Q. Do you still hope that you will be able to balance the budget by fiscal 1983?

A. I'm hoping, but you have got to remember that every percentage point of additional unemployment adds billions of dollars to the cost of Government and reduces Government revenues because of people no longer paying taxes.

Q. How would you try to reduce social welfare programs?

A. There is no question about maintaining the level of support for those people truly in need. But there can be a tightening up of regulations that make it legitimately possible for people of rather fair income to continue getting certain social welfare grants.

Q. Do you have any plans to back away at all from your intention to cut personal income taxes 10% a year for three years?

A. No.

Q. You have said that you were opposed only to environmental "extremism." What precisely do you mean by that?

A. When I use that term extremism, I mean a kind of literal translation of some of the regulations. For instance, you may find a demand for 100% purity of water. Now the streams you are turning that water into are not 100% pure, and in many instances the cost of getting up to 100% may be several times greater than the cost of getting to 95%. I think you have to have some realism about looking at something of that kind and saying wait a minute here.

Q. It is your desire to make the margins of these regulations more rational?

A. That's right. I prize clean air and clean water as much as anyone else. And certainly from the standpoint of preserving beauty, I am an environmentalist.

Q. But you are also an advocate of the so-called sagebrush rebellion that would turn federal lands in the West back to the states.

A. Yes. Because there I think the Federal Government has gone against the very principles of the Constitution. You must remember that the Federal Government was created by the states, not the other way around. And now [laughing] this monster the states have created is acting as the master over the states.

Q. But doesn't your experience as a Governor tell you that if a lot of acreage were turned back to the states, it would be much more vulnerable to rapid development because state governments are less able than Washington to withstand all of the pressure from business interests?

A. But are they? Just look at your own area. Look at California. Look at how easily even neighborhoods can stop a development. What makes us think Americans are more environmentally minded at the national level than they are at the state level? I just don't believe that. Now I also believe, however, that the Federal Government [has a role to play] with national parks and certain wilderness areas that are unique. They're not part of the sagebrush rebellion. I think there is a happy medium in which you preserve beauty, but to have a state in which 80% of the land belongs to the Federal Government does not make much sense.

Q. Moving on to foreign affairs, what do you think a Warsaw Pact invasion of Poland would do to East/West relations?

A. I think that the Soviet Union has got to be convinced that the results of such an action would be very severe. Now, you can ask yourself, how would the free world quarantine the Soviet Union with regard to trade and so forth? You have to ask yourself, can the Soviet Union exist on its own? It never has. The Soviet Union, with all its boastfulness about its system, could not live without support and help by way of trade and so forth from capitalist nations. If their system is so great, how come they're not self-sufficient? They are probably richer in minerals and fuel supplies than any other nation.

Q. So you think a quarantine might be one repercussion of an invasion?

A. It shows the possibilities. The Soviet Union is not as rich industrially as the rest of Europe. It has a smaller population than the rest of Europe. Maybe it's time for us to get out of this syndrome, if that's the proper word ... to stop thinking of the Soviets as being ten feet tall. They're not all that invulnerable.

Q. If the Soviets do not move on Poland, do you now have in mind even a rough timetable for arms control talks? Are you getting any signals from Brezhnev?

A. There is no way for me to outline a timetable on that. I have made it plain that I believe in legitimate negotiations that are aimed at reducing the strategic nuclear weapons in the world. I just think you cannot sit down at the negotiating table and ignore the policies of the Soviet Union, when you're talking disarmament, while they're carrying on as they are in Afghanistan and Africa and so forth.

Q. President Nixon introduced détente with the Soviets. As a Republican, do you think that in the eyes of the American public you would also have more leeway than a Democrat to deal with Moscow?

A. No, I don't think so. I could sum up in one sentence, I think, what I feel the attitude toward Russia should be. The Soviet empire should know that there will be no further concessions from us unless there is a concession in return.

Q. President Nixon has been in touch with you occasionally since the election. Do you expect to be discussing foreign policy with him periodically once you are in the White House?

A. I have not made any plans, but I would not rule it out. I think there is no question, if you look back at the record, about his knowledge of world affairs and world figures.

Q. Concerning the Middle East, do you plan to follow President Sadat's recommendation to call for a new summit meeting with yourself, Sadat and Prime Minister Begin?

A. Obviously, I don't want any retreat there on the part of our country. I want to make it plain to both Sadat and Prime Minister Begin that the United States does have an interest in the Middle East. We should not try to dictate a settlement, but be as helpful as we can in arriving at a settlement.

Q. You have expressed a good deal of interest in improving relations with Central America. What specifically should the U.S. be doing to help restore stability in the latest trouble spot, El Salvador?

A. I think that with regard to all of our neighbors to the south, we have been somewhat insensitive to our size and our power. We have gone at them with plans and proposals and with good intentions, but it appears to them that this is something in the nature of an order. Here is a plan. Accept it. I think it is time for us to approach them only with the idea that I think we all share, and that is that there must be a more practical and better relationship than we have had because of [a common] interest in freedom. Maybe our first approach should be to find out their suggestions. How can we mutually benefit each other? I look forward to trying that. Concerning El Salvador, I think that there is one thing you have to say about the situation there: it is almost a kind of civil war. When that is happening, and if reforms are needed—and admittedly reforms are needed—you do not try to fight a civil war and institute reforms at the same time. Get rid of the war. Then go forward with the reforms.

Q. Some foreign governments consider you to be less concerned than the Carter Administration about their handling of protest movements. How strongly should the U.S. push nations like those in Central America on human rights?

A. Well, first of all, of course, I'm for human rights. And I think that is an American position, and I do not think we will ever retreat from it or ever should. But I think we have to balance better than we have. We should not carry our campaign for human rights to some small country we can pressure to the point where a government that, let's say, partially violates human rights in our eyes is succeeded by a government that denies all human rights. For example, Cuba. There was no question about Batista, and violations there of human rights in our eyes. But can we say the people in Cuba are today better off than they were before? In no way. There are no human rights under Castro. There are no human rights under the Soviet Union, as we see them. Now how can we justify making every concession in the world to have détente with the Soviet Union at the same time that we use the mailed fist, you might say, against some smaller country that in some instances, faced with dissent, violates human rights? What I believe is that we do our utmost to bring about [improvement in human rights] in those countries that are aligned with us, but not at the expense of helping an overthrow by a [faction] that is totalitarian. Take South Korea as an example. The South Korean government is doing things that we do not support. We wish they could be different. Do we take an action that opens South Korea up to possible conquest by North Korea where, again, there are no human rights?

Q. You have often talked about what the Federal Government should not attempt to do. Yet you have also urged a return to "traditional values," to use your phrase. What role do you see yourself taking in the area of traditional values or social questions?

A. Well, I suppose that is in the context of what Teddy Roosevelt said about the White House being a bully pulpit. I think that all of our leaders, whether state, local or national, can have an impact by setting examples themselves, and trying to see that government is as high-principled as it can be, ending if possible this concept that most people in America now accept that there's a double standard—that you can accept things in politics that you would not accept in private business or your own dealings.

Q. Does use of the bully pulpit include using the President's prestige to promote constitutional amendments outlawing abortion in most circumstances and sanctioning prayer in public schools and that sort of thing?

A. Long before I ever sought this job, I believed that the outlawing of prayer, nonsectarian prayer, in public schools was not a defense of the First Amendment but was actually against the Constitution, which says that the Congress shall make no laws concerning the establishment of religion or the restriction of it or its practice and so forth. I just think [the restrictions] went too far. This is a nation under God. It is still on our coins: IN GOD WE TRUST. The Divine Providence is mentioned in our most important documents, the Declaration of Independence and the Constitution. As for abortion, I think it is a constitutional question. The [advocates] of the right of abortion speak of the right of a mother or a prospective mother and her own body. We are talking of two bodies.

Q. One thing that set your campaign apart from many others is that you always seemed to maintain a very healthy sense of humor out there on the road. Even when things were not going well. Are you going to continue to do that?

A. Yes. I think I'm very fortunate that I can find occasion to laugh even when the situation may not warrant it.

Q. Or, perhaps more important, help your audience, which is now the whole country and the whole world, to laugh?

A. You know, you can quote Lincoln on that. Lincoln said that if he had lost the ability to laugh during the terrible times in which he presided, he could not have gone on—that the job would have been intolerable. I think one of the great compliments to Americans was given by Winston Churchill in the dark days of World War II when he said of American soldiers that they seemed to be the only people who could laugh and fight at the same time.

My Reagan Road Trip

SEPARATING MAN FROM MYTH

BY BOB SPITZ

Bob Spitz is best known for his biographies of such popular figures as Julia Child and Bob Dylan. He is now working on a biography of Ronald Reagan. As part of his research, he has begun visiting locations in the U.S. and abroad that were pivotal in Reagan's life.

YOU HAD TO LOOK HARD TO SEE THE CARDBOARD sign in the window of the abandoned First National Bank: "Birthplace of President Ronald Reagan." I'd cruised through the town twice, head swiveling, before it finally caught my eye. It's indicative of how my search for Reagan was unfolding. After nearly two years, researching what I hoped would be the definitive biography of the beloved 40th president, I'd stumbled upon a setting that was humbling, and the weight of my task began to sink in. Writing a major biography of Ronald Reagan was going to require a Homeric effort to separate the man from the myth.

In his own day, Reagan was larger than life, but also a mystery unpenetrated by even his closest friends. He was intensely private, personally inaccessible, some say a cipher, who has eluded several estimable biographers to date. All true enough, but what a fabulously intriguing subject.

For me, the story has everything—an up-from-the-bootstraps Midwestern adolescence; a foray into the golden age of radio broadcasting; a Hollywood scenario featuring an unparalleled cast of stars; divorce, American style; Red Scare intrigue at the heart of the House Un-American Activities Committee; a startling shift into politics; an assassination attempt; a once-unimaginable campaign that netted him the most important role on the world stage. Toss into this the rise of modern conservatism, plus the fall of the Iron Curtain, and you have a biography that evokes a full-scale 20th-century tableau.

But on top of all that, I was keen to know what drove Reagan. What enabled him to have such an enormous impact on our culture? These questions, among others, inspired me to embark on an investigative odyssey of my own. In addition to burying myself in archives and library stacks, I set out to retrace the man's steps.

As someone who linked his appeal to the values of the heartland, Reagan's feet were firmly planted there. My search for those roots began in Tampico, Ill., a blink-and-you-miss-it hamlet just off the Hennepin Canal, where Reagan was born and spent the early years of his life. The whole of the town could fit inside a midsize Walmart. The place wasn't much to look at—no cherry tree for chopping down, not even a stoplight to brake one's progress on the way to somewhere else. A smattering of redbrick storefronts joined at the shoulder sat hard by one side of the blocklong South Main Street where that innocuous sign in the window of the abandoned bank alerted passersby to Reagan's birthplace upstairs.

I followed a woman who curates the premises up a narrow staircase into a warren of somber rooms. Little money was available for decorating the modest flat, but Nelle Reagan, Ronald's mother, brightened it with floral wallpaper, a few small framed prints and sheer lace curtains, sewn by hand, that welcomed the sunlight. From the front parlor, a formal no-man's-land reserved for company, I could see across to the corner building, now a shabby bar, where Jack Reagan, Ronald's father, sold dry goods at H.C. Pitney's general store. Beyond it a monolithic grain silo reached skyward like a Mercury rocket. Gone was Burden's Opera House, where Jack and Nelle performed in treacly morality plays and Jack mimed in blackface revues. Gone were the bakery, grocery and butcher shop, the cornerstones of community. And gone was any sign of Tampico youth, who made beelines to Chicago, St. Louis, Indianapolis, Kansas City—anywhere else—at the first chance.

Later, in 1919, when the Reagans returned to town, they relocated to a flat above the Pitney store, seriously cramped quarters for a family raising two rambunctious boys, with an outdoor toilet, always an adventure. But there were ideal places to play: miles of hard-packed bicycle paths, the pens of the town stockyards and an alley behind their old apartment whose garbage cans supplied ammunition for the boys' regular food fights.

It was hard to imagine somebody from this modest background one day walking in the corridors of power. I got a more tangible sense of Reagan when I arrived in Dixon, roughly 30 miles to the north, where he spent the bulk of his formative years. Dixon is appealing, accessible and conservative, which is indicative of the man Reagan was to become. "All of us have to have a place to go back to," he wrote in an early memoir. "Dixon is that place for me."

To a poor boy from Tampico, Dixon must have seemed full of promise. Situated on a scenic bend of the Rock River, it was a forward-looking city, with bustling mills, a convergence of major U.S. rail lines, and crowded movie houses, where the hero always prevailed. The Dixon Theater still stands on South Galena Avenue, where the town's future movie star watched Tom Mix two-reelers and famously boycotted *The Birth of a Nation*.

The Reagan homestead, a handsome white frame place at 816 S. Hennepin Avenue, was built around the turn of the century, with a proper front porch, indoor plumbing and a large, airy kitchen at the back with a zinc sink and two oak iceboxes. A dark cubbyhole off the kitchen had held a single bed that Ronald shared with his older brother, Neil. The back porch, where the boys slept on sticky summer nights, overlooked Nelle's vegetable garden and a garage where the boys raised rabbits.

Reagan, whom everyone called Dutch, took his cue from Dixon's warm, unguarded citizenry and those gutsy white-hatted warriors up on the screen. He taught Sunday school at the First Christian Church on Hennepin Avenue, acted in dramatic-club plays and manned the lifeguard's chair in leafy Lowell Park, the cynosure of dozy summer days. His role was simple: if people got in trouble he saved them, like Brass Bancroft, the Secret Service agent he later portrayed in a series of low-budget movies. Nothing was more straightforward. He kept order with the power of his presence, even if a local lass or two fluttered foxily in the water in hopes of catching his eye.

Reagan drew his strong moral core from Dixon. The spirit of heroic idealism and enterprise that appealed to him as president remains evident everywhere in the city, from its well-trodden football fields to the well-kept front porches to the riverbank streets, where townsfolk still gather on Saturday nights to socialize and trade the latest gossip. There were annual Chautauquas at Assembly Park, and parades galore that passed under the stately War Memorial Arch. Amid the crushing hardships of Depression-era life, Dixon, for Reagan, was an oasis of stability.

It's somewhat easier to visualize him in Des Moines, Iowa, where he landed in 1933, a year after graduating from Eureka College. Des Moines was the city that sparked his dreams, with its 22 movie theaters, supercharged political atmosphere and vibrant nightlife that offered him a taste of celebrity. In Des Moines, Reagan developed a lasting persona. Radio WHO, a 50,000-watt station where he broke in as a sportscaster, was the unarguable voice of the Midwest, and Dutch Reagan one of its rising young stars. Actually, celebrity was more like it. His husky voice became an embraceable signature. From a small studio on the ground floor of the Stoner Piano Building on Walnut Street, Reagan broadcast Chicago Cubs games he re-created from transcripts as they came in over the Teletype. "Lon Warneke is dusting his hands in the resin, steps back up on the mound, is getting the sign again from Hartnett—here's the windup and the pitch ..." One can almost see him sitting curled over the microphone in full-blown performance, shoulders punctuating each breathtaking play, as he described action occurring hundreds of miles away. If one seeks to pinpoint the origin of the Great Communicator, it was there, in that windowless room in Des Moines.

For Dutch Reagan, success had its own rewards. He slipped easily from his role as nascent choirboy to that of man about town, making the rounds of the fashionable Des Moines night scene. His repertoire followed an established circuit: cocktails at Cy's Moonlight Inn, dinner at the Kirkwood, the floor show at Club Belvedere. I tried to imagine him pulling up to each establishment—all long gone, sad to say—in his Nash LaFayette convertible, a revolving cast of beauties clinging to an arm. Or forcing himself awake the next morning in time for an early swim or horseback ride in the park at Camp Dodge.

But Des Moines couldn't contain a meteor like Dutch Reagan. It felt almost natural to follow him out west, because California—Hollywood—was the logical next stop. As soon as Reagan got a taste of the spotlight, it was inevitable he would head straight there. The glare was too seductive. And the Warner Bros. lot was the brightest light in town, home to the most dazzling stars: James Cagney, Barbara Stanwyck, Edward G. Robinson, Bette Davis, Joan Blondell, Paul Muni, Rin Tin Tin.

Reagan's screen test was a fait accompli. He had charisma, sex appeal and a willingness to play by the restrictive studio rules of the era. For a biographer, the movies he made offer a rich overview of the strong, decent, masculine American, Hollywood version. From the time Reagan pulled on a swimsuit or sweet-talked a radio audience, he had laid the foundation of an image that would one day fulfill a longing for strong and decent leaders. And under the Warner Bros. aegis, he further burnished the role of the American hero and learned the essentials of performance, which became ever more crucial in politics in the media age.

Here in California, Reagan began in earnest to forge the epic story of his life. His own voyage is taking me up and down the California coastline, where he made his home in an assortment of mansions and ranches. I'm still at sea in my ongoing research, but I have an itinerary that has me hopscotching around the globe—to Sacramento and the White House; to Geneva, where he met Mikhail Gorbachev; to Checkpoint Charlie in Berlin, where he precipitated the dismantling of the wall; to Chernobyl, Reykjavik, Grenada and the Middle East.

With each stop, I will gauge the significance of these historic places, but, more important, I will search in every instance for the essence of the man—the qualities, the temperament, the inner struggles, that led him from an unassuming background to such extraordinary influence over our culture and beyond. From Tampico to the pinnacle of the free world, Reagan's story came to define more than one man's odyssey—it came, for many, to define our age.

TIME

MANAGING EDITOR Nancy Gibbs
CREATIVE DIRECTOR D.W. Pine
DIRECTOR OF PHOTOGRAPHY Kira Pollack

The Reagan Paradox
The Conservative Icon and Today's GOP

EDITOR Robert F. Howe

DESIGNERS Elaine Ahn, Anne-Michelle Gallero, Heather Haggerty

PHOTO EDITOR Patricia Cadley

CONTRIBUTORS Alex Altman, Michael Beschloss, Lou Cannon, Michael Duffy, Jon Meacham, Molly Moore, Landon Parvin, Joe Scarborough, Craig Shirley, Bob Spitz

COPY EDITOR David Olivenbaum

REPORTER Mary Alice Shaughnessy

EDITORIAL PRODUCTION David Sloan

TIME HOME ENTERTAINMENT PUBLISHER Jim Childs VICE PRESIDENT AND ASSOCIATE PUBLISHER Margot Schupf VICE PRESIDENT, FINANCE Vandana Patel EXECUTIVE DIRECTOR, MARKETING SERVICES Carol Pittard EXECUTIVE DIRECTOR, BUSINESS DEVELOPMENT Suzanne Albert EXECUTIVE DIRECTOR, MARKETING Susan Hettleman PUBLISHING DIRECTOR Megan Pearlman ASSOCIATE DIRECTOR OF PUBLICITY Courtney Greenhalgh ASSISTANT GENERAL COUNSEL Simone Procas ASSISTANT DIRECTOR, SPECIAL SALES Ilene Schreider SENIOR MARKETING MANAGER, SALES MARKETING Danielle Costa SENIOR MANAGER, CATEGORY MARKETING Bryan Christian ASSOCIATE PRODUCTION MANAGER Kimberly Marshall ASSOCIATE PREPRESS MANAGER Alex Voznesenskiy ASSISTANT PROJECT MANAGER Hillary Hirsch EDITORIAL DIRECTOR Stephen Koepp SENIOR EDITOR Roe D'Angelo COPY CHIEF Rina Bander DESIGN MANAGER Anne-Michelle Gallero EDITORIAL OPERATIONS Gina Scauzillo SPECIAL THANKS Katherine Barnet, Brad Beatson, Jeremy Biloon, Rose Cirrincione, Assu Etsubneh, Mariana Evans, Christine Font, David Kahn, Jean Kennedy, Amy Mangus, Courtney Mifsud, Nina Mistry, Dave Rozzelle, Matthew Ryan, Ricardo Santiago, Divyam Shrivastava, Adriana Tierno